EQ/IQ

Developing Emotional Intelligence for Effective Executive Support

Melba J. Duncan
with Emily Schatz, Tim Shea,
and Loretta Sophocleous

Melba J. Duncan
EQ/IQ: Developing Emotional Intelligence
for Effective Executive Support

Open Hand Press, March 2021
ISBN: 978-1-7340321-3-0

"Melba Duncan is quite simply an icon of the administrative profession. When she speaks, you can hear a pin drop. The audience hangs on her every word. Nobody understands the role of the EA better than Melba. The World Economic Forum's 'Future of Jobs Report 2018' cite Emotional Intelligence as being one of the top 10 skills of the future and it is, without doubt one of an EA's greatest assets. This book is a 'must read' for any career EA looking to gain a greater understanding of the importance of EQ to the role or to upskill and future proof their career."

  – **Lucy Brazier** – CEO, Marcham Publishing, Publisher of *Executive Secretary Magazine*, International Speaker

"Whether you're already in an EA role, considering becoming an EA, or contemplating hiring an EA, this book is for you. The author 'owns' this space, you'll be learning from the best. As Melba makes explicitly clear, being an EA is one of the most demanding, yet satisfying, experiences any professional could ever hope for."

  – **Bill Wiersma**, Author of *The Power of Professionalism*, and *The Power of Identity*.

"Brilliant! *EQ/IQ* is an important achievement and one that will make significant waves in the new workplace. Once again, Melba J. Duncan shows that she knows things that leaders need to know and is fearless to say the truths that need to be said. What Melba knows is that Executive Life Managers are essential to the success of business and that the smartest leaders need to fully leverage one of the ELM's greatest innate skills – EQ. From her 40+ year career, Melba J. Duncan has such a deep well of experience, combined with the ability to articulate the unspoken truths that have serious bottom line impact on companies. When Melba talks, leaders listen, because what she says is their secret to success. And when she writes a book like *EQ/IQ*, they will read every word."

     – **Bonnie Low-Kramen**, Author, *Be the Ultimate Assistant*

"No one knows the true scope and dynamic of the Executive/ Assistant partnership like Melba J. Duncan, the most respected voice in this profession. *EQ/IQ* should be required reading by both the executive and their assistant as a playbook for building an effective, influential, and successful partnership. Grab your highlighter. Brainstorm ideas. Develop a plan of action. Save years of trial and error and achieve your organization's business objectives together, faster."

     – **Vickie Sokol Evans**, RedCape Founder/CEO

"Melba has worked at the highest level of executive support prior to her second career as Founder of The Duncan Group in New York City. This experience affords her a deep and rich perspective for her work. She is also a visionary with extremely well-developed EQ/IQ herself. She is driven by both the highest devotion to service and excellence and manages both with warmth and unparalleled professionalism. Very simply, I consider Melba Duncan to be the "gold standard" of our profession. I am honored to endorse her new book.

     – **Leni Miller**, Founder and President, EASearch, LLC. Author of *Finding Right Work, Five Steps to a Life You Love.*

"Melba Duncan is one of the foremost thought leaders and visionaries for the executive support profession. She knows firsthand what it means to be an effective executive assistant, and I've learned so much from her throughout my EA career. I work in the artificial intelligence space, and I believe cultivating our emotional intelligence is one of the best tactics for future-proofing our role. Melba's book is a must read for administrative professionals (and their executives) who don't want to be left behind.

- **Jeremy Burrows**, Author of *The Leader Assistant: Four Pillars of a Confident, Game-Changing Assistant.* Host of the #1 podcast for assistants – 'The Leader Assistant Podcast.'

"Gone are the days of the executive assistant who just brings the boss a coffee or keeps their calendar. Thank goodness! Unfortunately, this stereotype still exists and impacts the value of the role and the possibilities for growth and upward mobility in many organizations. Melba, Loretta and Tim provide a compelling approach for helping executive assistants leverage their technical and soft skills, elevate their brand, and become a trusted business partner. Now is the time to act. Make an investment in yourself and learn from these experts. Create the new reality of the role and one that will be valued no matter the disruptor!"

- **Bridget Sarikas**, Partner, L3 Fusion LLC and Vice President, Right Advisory LLC, Co-author of *Stupid Gone Viral – When Science and Reality Collide*

"*EQ/IQ* is a must read for all executive assistants who strive for maximum professional performance. Melba

Duncan has created a blueprint for understanding what it takes to be in a dynamic partnership with an executive or CEO. Her latest book offers a compelling framework and fresh insights on how to be a high-performing individual in this uniquely rewarding role."

- **Norma Tan**, Organizational Consultant, Cora Group, Inc.

"I have worked with Tim Shea for close to twenty years. I've come to know him as a conscientious, deeply caring individual. Tim is a deep thinker. It's important to him to truly understand the other person. He is a prolific asker of questions and is a contemplative listener. Absorb, learn, and benefit from his shared knowledge."

- **Garry Terhune**, Sales Presentations Coach

Acknowledgements

This book acknowledges the vitality, intelligence, innovative skills, and perseverance exemplified by the Global Professional Executive Assistant. This is a population that expands its workplace contribution with a tenacity of purpose.

I confirm my gratitude to global business leaders, who have offered us the opportunity to learn from and work with them while managing their recruiting and training requirements.

Thank you to my contributing writers – Emily Schatz, Tim Shea, and Loretta Sophocleous – who personify the mastery of Emotional Intelligence and effective communication.

A very special thanks to my daughter, Michelle K. Oosterwal, for her kindness and brilliance. For being the best part of my life. For being the mother of my grandchildren, Francesca and Angelica. For her acumen as a business partner, together we expand The Duncan Group, Inc. to reflect her commitment to achievement.

This acknowledgement allows me to express my sincerest appreciation for Max Rodriguez, our publisher, and the editorial team of Louis Birro and Lead Editor, Julio Mendez, whose talent is apparent in the management of this process. Together, they represent mastery.

Friends and colleagues, such as Diane L. Rush and Noreen P. Denihan, have been an encouragement and steadfast inspiration. I thank you for reminding me that dreams never go out of business.

Table of Contents

TABLE OF CONTENTS
EQ /IQ CASE STORIES

EQ/IQ

Developing Emotional Intelligence for Effective Executive Support

Melba J. Duncan
with Emily Schatz, Tim Shea,
and Loretta Sophocleous

The Power of Competency:
Skills Sustain an Organization

Do you know that Executives and Executive Assistants are fated to the same result? Why? Because we are in a global competitive battle: workplace collaboration, with a focus on workplace diversity, plays a key role in global business survival. And the powerful impact of technology and global communication encourages the premise that fewer workers are necessary. This exerts pressure on the need to expand our capabilities.

A broad understanding of how global business works is the Executive Assistant's competitive advantage. This presents both a great opportunity and a real challenge to the Executive Assistant, as it defines the unique transitions in the role.

Here are some of the ongoing changing conditions that are positively transforming this position:

1. Evolving social media: the popularity of social media and blog posts confirm that we are a culture that prefers information in short bursts.

2. Threats to cyber-security: web security.

3. Compliance with new regulatory requirements in the United States and similar regulatory schemes in the rest of the world.

4. Increasing importance and time required to develop relationships with global division Executives (and their Assistants) whose businesses are often the fastest growing in a company.

5. Engagement in legislative debates and politics as Executives increasingly participate in the political process to secure their company's interests.

These are not simple challenges. Yet, as businesses and Executives grapple with this new world, so, too, must Executive Assistants "up their game" to compete globally. We must state with unconditional exactness that the urgent priority of today's global Assistant is to apply discipline and focus to day-to-day tasks and to solve problems while keeping Executives informed of important circumstances. Most relevant is the ability of the Assistant to understand the personal and business context of the Executive, within which he or she must manage the imperative and diverse responsibilities of the role.

Today's innovative business model requires that the very best talent be sourced, engaged, developed, and retained. The measure of Executive Assistant success will depend upon whether you have a balanced outlook for both the short and the long term. Global Executive Assistants: your success depends on how you assess and respond to global business and to Executive needs, and how you align your strategy with that of the Executive and your company's mission.

I remain deeply passionate and proud of my background as an Executive Assistant. This experience confirms that there is no better way to understand the nuance of the role and the significance of the Executive/ Executive Assistant Business Partnership. The following experience remains a vivid memory:

I arrive ten minutes ahead of time for my interview with the CEO. I am directed to an exquisitely designed boardroom with plush seating for 20, paneled walls, everything quite still. I move nervously from chair to chair to choose my most advantageous position. This is a serious, no-distraction environment, I think. I decide upon the seat at the right of the head of the table. Almost immediately, the doors swing open and, in a blur, the Executive crosses the boardroom and sits in what seems to be his accustomed chair at the other end of the table. I slide into the chair opposite him.

"Is that how fast I can expect you to move in getting my work done or in making a decision?" Before I could answer, he continues, "I am tough, demanding, and unable to tolerate ill-advised mistakes. Why would you want this job?"

"I am also tough, demanding, and unable to tolerate ill-advised mistakes," I was able to interject, "and that is why I can do this job."

He stood up and turned, just long enough to say: "Tell whoever it is that you talk to in HR that you are hired. By the way, what is your name?"

"Melba Duncan" I responded, as he vanished through the closing door. Three weeks later, I reported for my first real job assisting Sanford C. Bernstein, CEO, Sanford C. Bernstein & Company. From this experience, I learned the vital foundation skills of Executive support, and most importantly, how to work with challenging personalities.

The next milestone event in my career, with the most memorable lessons, was my role as the Executive

Assistant to The Honorable Peter G. Peterson, CEO of Lehman Brothers. I held that position for 10 years. I recall an event where there was a luncheon to be held for the then Secretary of State: my responsibility is to send out invites with names, titles, addresses – no errors – and create the master list; I am then to keep track of RSVPs, and check every detail (names, spelling, titles, etc.) over and over again. The request from Pete is to have the room set up with "horseshoe" seating: Okay, I think; then ask myself, what does that mean?

Pete asks that I also design the seating arrangements for his review. Done. In the meantime, menus must be printed with the final guest list attached. All must be proofread, brought to the printer, picked up, and proofed again, before the final print run. 9:00 p.m.; relief – they are all done. 9:05 p.m., I receive a phone call: "Melba, yes? I just received a call that Mr. X. cannot be there. Can we delete his name from the final list?" Perfect.

Wasting no time, I call the printer: "If we do this," he says, "you can't get it until tomorrow at 10:00 a.m." I weep. Lunch is at 12:00 noon. Do not panic, I think to myself, just put a plan into action. Okay… *I* will pick them up. *I* will take a cab, pick up the final list from the printer (after having proofread against the master list), and continue uptown by cab to the lunch venue, with enough time for me to place name cards before everyone arrives. Done.

Of course, come morning, it is raining, and I am drenched. The cab waits while I retrieve the list, we crawl uptown, and I fly out of the cab into the Executive Club.

The Maitre d' looks at me oddly, then asks: "Where are you going?" "To the 'X' Room," I answer. "Well," he replies, "women are not allowed in that room." Tears well up; it is now 11:45 a.m. "I am only arranging the place cards," I explain. "Sorry," he says.

"Me too," I respond, apologizing as I rush into the room to distribute the place cards. As I put the last card in place, the first guests, Pete and the then-Secretary of State, arrive. Pete looks at me, the first woman in this venerable room. I look back at him, smile and I just keep walking. I shouldn't have been there, we both knew that; but I needed to be... so I was. At that moment, I learned the importance of commitment to a task, concern and respect for others, of friendship, and of bypassing all obstacles to get the job done.

Those experiences, and my 35 subsequent years in the business of matching Executive Assistants with CEOs worldwide, tell me that neither the stereotype of a 1960s Mad Men Secretary, nor of the modern-day Assistant, embrace the true scope, range, and nuance of this essential position. Neither projection allows for, or acknowledges, the integral and integrated Business Partnership that is fueled by the Executive/Executive Assistant team's reach for success in today's increasingly competitive global economy.

In my work placing Executive Assistants and Chiefs of Staff globally, I meet regularly with CEOs. In those discussions, I have learned that they expect their Assistants to connect their role to opportunities in technology, as well as with rapid global and social changes. This means that Assistants will make better decisions that are based more on knowledge and competence than on their position in an organizational hierarchy.

Many of the job descriptions we review flatly disagree with the data we have gathered about the traits, attitudes, and specialized skills that are now required. There is no single agreed-upon description of what this position entails, or even agreement on appropriate titles. In practice, the tremendous variations among administrative professional roles arise from the different motives behind creating the position.

To understand where we are now, here are a few career evolutions that you may want to contemplate that challenge the popular perception of this role. Here is what you need to know: Today's professional Assistant must be smart in the ways that the Executive is not. You must exemplify resourcefulness, teamwork, social skills, digital sophistication, flexibility, tenacity, optimism, a yearning for new learning, and a global outlook. You must envision yourself as a catalyst: you must deliver successful business outcomes (you have the capacity to understand and to process and analyze enormous amounts of data, and you make no assumptions). The quality of your decisions is what makes you valuable; so, you must have the analytical capacity to understand what is important and to apply creativity to the challenges encountered.

A great realization towers above all others: Just about everyone needs a reliable, experienced, Executive Assistant. The Executive Assistant is a very special breed of individual. You are more than enduring! You are always confident, team-oriented, and multi-faceted. You are indispensable in the digital/virtual workforce!

In light of all this, how does the Executive Assistant exemplify leadership, which is defined by the ability to motivate and inspire others to respond positively to change; to demonstrate self-sustaining skills strategy and thereby communicate with positive energy the new relevance of this profession? To answer this, you must first answer the question: Who do you become when things go wrong?

Executive Support: The Profession That Evolves at the Speed of Business

by Loretta Sophocleous

The C-Suite Executive Assistant position is unique and distinct in many ways. It is a partnership that transcends the more typical support-based positions known as "Executive Assistant." There is much confusion as to specific duties and responsibilities of the C-Suite Executive Assistant since the title is currently used for a plethora of other more administrative functions. Unfortunately, this leads to incorrect information regarding the job description, compensation, and required skills.

Many Executives in the business world do not totally understand this distinction. Executive Assistants are so skilled in what they do, that Executives do not question what they *are* doing – they only know that their needs and requests are met successfully. Fault is also found in the fact that many Executive Assistants are not educating Executives regarding what they are bringing to the table. Most employees in this profession are comfortable remaining in the background to propel those they work for to be successful. That is not a problem. The problem lies in the fact that all categories of Executive Assistants are lumped into one big bucket, from clerical assistant to chiefs of staff, thereby skewing important statistics.

I remember reading an article a few years ago regarding a very important Executive and his Executive Assistant who was a combination of partner, support person, conscience, and advisor; a very valued and trusted partner to the Executive; however, later in the article it noted that the median salary for an Executive Assistant was $60,000! Well, certainly not at that level! At that level, we are talking about six figures. This exemplifies the danger of lumping together all levels of the profession, which creates inaccurate statistics.

The C-Suite Executive Assistant needs to be classified correctly. It is evident that there is a huge discrepancy, even within the United States Department of Labor, for these positions. Eth Lloyd, a respected Executive Assistant advocate, provided a survey of Executive Assistants attending the 2018 World Administrative Summit that revealed a wide range of titles used to identify the Executive Assistant. I have listed several of those (*by all means, not complete!*) - alphabetically - to give clarity to the abounding confusion. Here are a few: Administrative Assistant, Administrative Coordinator, Administrative Manager, Administrative Services Manager, Administrative Services Officer, Administrative Specialist, Administrative Support Manager, Administrative Support Supervisor, Administrator, Assistant Director, Chief of Staff, Director of Administrative Services, Executive Advisor, Executive Assistant, Executive Personal Assistant, Executive Services Administrator, Executive Strategic Partner, Human Resources Administrator, Lead Executive Assistant, Legal Secretary, Office Administrator, Personal Assistant, Program Administrator, Program Manager, Secretary, Senior Administrative Coordinator, Senior Administrative Services Officer, Senior Executive

Assistant, Senior Executive Business Partner, Senior Special Events Coordinator, Senior Support Assistant, Senior Support Specialist, Special Assistant to the _____, Special Events Coordinator, and Vice-President of Administration. A veritable smorgasbord of titles...!

Upon informing the Department of Labor of this confusion of titles, the response was that the next re-evaluation of the job was to occur in 2028! Thankfully, many of the salary survey companies have better intel as to appropriate compensation at different levels but, even so, clarity is needed. The only way this can occur is by educating the business world, the leaders of industry, CHROs, etc. We all need to help in that effort.

Continuing education is key at this level. If we are to be true partners to Executives, we need to know what they know – we need to seek out subject matter that is relevant to the business. And we need to understand that we are just as important to the business as to Executives; therefore, we seek out these opportunities. I am dismayed when I hear an Executive Assistant say that he or she is not important enough to merit the expense to the company for a seminar or conference. By choosing the appropriate venue for learning, you are enhancing what you do for the Executive and for the company.

It is important that this position is understood for what it truly is. Unfortunately, it has been too long in coming. We are on the road to changing that now...

"What the Heck is Water?" An Introduction to Emotional Intelligence
– by Tim Shea

In a 2005 commencement speech at Kenyon College, the writer David Foster Wallace famously told the following story: Two young fish are swimming along when they are passed by an older fish. The older fish says, "Hello there, folks. How's the water today?" The two young fish continue swimming but, after a little while, one fish turns to the other and says, "...What the heck is *water*?"

Sometimes we are so immersed in something, it is so much a part of our everyday experience, that we do not notice it is there. Emotional Intelligence is like that... it is a set of reference points that we use to navigate our relationship with ourselves and others. Those reference points have always been there, we just haven't noticed much.

We will use the term EQ (as in Emotional Quotient) when referring to Emotional Intelligence. EQ is the term we will use going forward.

So, what, exactly, is EQ?

When you name something, it comes into being. In 1990, **two psychologists, John D.** Mayer and Peter Salovey, coined the term "Emotional Intelligence," describing it as a form of social intelligence. Mayer and Salovey initiated research to develop valid measures of emotional intelligence and explore its significance. Daniel Goleman, who was then a science writer for the *New York Times*, followed their work with great interest and in 1995 published his book, *Emotional Intelligence - Why It Can Matter More Than IQ*, which became an international bestseller. EQ was on the map.

Emotional Intelligence can be defined as the ability to recognize, understand, and manage your emotions and the emotions of others to a positive outcome. Put simply, EQ helps us to work with people more effectively - it is the water in which we swim. EQ helps us to be less reactive and more responsive in our personal and professional lives.

A standard model of EQ illustrates 4 dimensions:

- **Self-Awareness** (Being aware of the rich array of feelings, sensations, states, thoughts, resources, and intuition we may have at any given moment)

- **Self-Management** (Using that awareness to understand and manage our internal state, resources, and impulses)

- **Social Awareness** (Empathically sensing and observing the behavior of others)

- **Relationship Management** (Using this awareness and understanding to navigate the moment-to-moment "give and take" in relationships and inducing desirable responses)

An advantage that EQ provides, that is not as readily provided by IQ, is *working effectively with people*. This sounds simplistic until you begin to reflect that most of our difficulties at work, and in our careers, are not because we lack subject matter expertise or technical skill but more often because we are not adept at the people/relational dimension of work. Communication leads to conflict rather than collaboration. Our negative emotions and poor relationship skills outshine our productive contribution. Our success takes a hit.

The development of EQ arose, in part, from that observation - why are smart people not always successful? Success was due to other abilities. You can be brilliant in your domain of knowledge, but your effectiveness will be limited by your ability to get others to work with you. The people we like to work with and who help us to go above and beyond are not necessarily the smartest folks in the room, but they may be the savviest.

If I asked you to describe the persons who brought out the best in you, you would probably say things like "They listened," or "They were patient," or "They challenged me..." These are all personal qualities of *being*. Who they were had a bigger impact than what they knew technically.

EQ increases trust, psychological safety, willingness to take risks, and the ability to give and receive feedback, among many other things. A distinct aspect of EQ is that it can grow through intention and focus. This is not true of IQ. IQ is a measure of abstract thinking, logical reasoning, mathematical ability, and spatial recognition. Your IQ score stabilizes in your early 20s and does not grow much beyond that. EQ grows throughout your entire life.

The psychologist, Edward de Bono, coined the term "lateral thinking." By that, he means deliberate creative thinking in order to create value by seeing something new. De Bono characterizes our standard modes of thinking, as originated by Aristotle, Socrates and Plato, as a logical-rational-linear search for the truth. Lateral thinking is an indirect and creative approach to see what is not immediately obvious. It involves seeing beyond and outside our default sense of the world.

There is a dimension of EQ that applies here. Seeing more, creating a larger, more-inclusive frame, sensing and responding with all of our capacity gives us insights beyond what is available to the intellect in isolation.

EQ expands our awareness. EQ provides access to breakthroughs in the same way that lateral thinking generates new perspectives and ideas. This additional capacity creates the possibility of much greater success and satisfaction.

Why EQ for Executive Assistants?

The Executive Assistant role has some inherent characteristics that are distinct from other roles. The role is both broader and less well-defined than other positions. It also typically has higher visibility and impact because the Executive Assistant is often supporting a significant player in the organization. Additionally, the individual qualities of the Assistant come into sharper focus because the Executive Assistant is supporting Executives on a personal level, not just how they function in their roles.

All of this requires increased levels of sensitivity, flexibility, and resilience. The Executive Assistant must remain steady and calm in moments of chaos and conflict, must get used to dealing with the unexpected with grace and resourcefulness, and must develop a clearer sense of boundaries.

Some Executive Assistants perform magic; they can see around corners and read minds. Emotional Intelligence has a distinct payoff when dealing with all the complexity, ambiguity, urgency and stress inherent in the Executive Assistant role. As stated above, EQ increases our ability to work effectively with people. Simply being less reactive and more responsive helps the Executive Assistant shine in moments of crisis. That ability to perform with poise and precision in pressured situations is a career-advancing quality.

Jack Welch, former CEO of GE, says, "A leader's intelligence has to have a strong emotional component. He has to have high levels of self-awareness, maturity and self-control. She must be able to withstand the heat, handle setbacks and when those lucky moments arise, enjoy success with equal parts of joy and humility. No doubt emotional intelligence is rarer than book smarts, but my experience says it is actually more important in the making of a leader. You just can't ignore it." Emotional Intelligence is a foundational skill because it enhances success in many work roles and environments.

A couple of examples: Sales agents at L'Oreal selected on the basis of certain emotional competencies significantly outsold other salespeople who were selected using the company's standard selection procedure for salespeople. On an annual basis, salespeople selected on the basis of emotional competence sold $91,370 more than did other salespeople, for a net revenue increase of $2,558,360.

A Komatsu manufacturing plant in Italy faced serious problems in the midst of a global recession, especially in terms of low employee engagement. Komatsu partnered with an EQ consulting company, Six Seconds, to develop a program for its plant managers blending assessments, training and project-based learning, all aimed at improving the climate. The results were a remarkable increase in engagement of 112%, coupled with an increase in plant performance of 9.4%.

The US Air Force reduced recruiter turnover from

35% annually to 5% annually by selecting candidates high in emotional intelligence. A $10,000 investment in EQ training realized a total cost savings of $3 million per year (GAO Archive).

Coca-Cola saw division leaders who developed EQ competencies outperform their targets by more than 15%. Division leaders who did not develop their EQ missed targets by the same margin (McClelland, 1999).

So, what can you do to increase your EQ? This book is threaded throughout with straightforward and practical actions you can take to grow your EQ. A few of my favorites:

Slow down. Become more aware of your physical sensations and emotions when there is conflict. Resist the impulse to speed up and just...*slow*...*down*.

Be curious. Cultivate an interest in the perspective of the other person. Ask questions, explore options, and get them to open up *before* you respond.

Empathize. Empathy is feeling *with* people. Improve your ability to see and feel things from their point of view. Identify their emotions and resist judgment.

Listen. Author Stephen Covey said, "Most people do not listen with the intent to understand, they listen with the intent to reply." The quality of your listening actually shapes the quality of their communication on a moment-to-moment basis.

As you will see, these suggestions are interrelated. Work on one dimension of the EQ/IQ model tends to improve other dimensions. End-of-chapter pointers, titled Sixty-Second Leadership©, provided throughout the book will be specific and, when you practice them, contagious. Make good use of the content found within the Case Story and their Toolkits, Takeaways, and Applications written by Emily Schatz. The information within this book, the Case Story, the end-of-book references and resources, and Melba's chapter-by-chapter webinar discussion will help set your compass toward a more effective you.

CHAPTER I

The Complex Nature of The Role

Jeff Bezos, American entrepreneur, Founder and Chief Executive Officer of Amazon, once said, "Your brand is what people say about you when you are not in the room." It is from this idea that I ask the question: What is the brand recognition that defines the strategic profile of the Executive Assistant? Simply put, it is the Power of Competence.

Four pillars support the Power of Competence of the Executive Assistant. They are Intuition, Initiative, Innovation and Integrity. And these essential attributes are tested for authenticity by the effectiveness and strength of seven distinctive characteristics: 1) implicit knowledge, 2) self-discipline, 3) intellectual and social understanding, 4) emotional recognition, 5) a positive attitude, 6) the patience to learn new skills, and 7) a willingness to try new ideas in order to respond to ever-changing circumstances. These strengths serve a compelling objective, which is to unlock the creativity of Executive Assistants so that they realize their greatest performance impact.

Let's think about these attributes that lead Executive Assistants to brand recognition and accountable results.

Intuition: By this, I mean the ability to see what is going to happen before it occurs. And how, exactly, do you do that? By understanding the thinking and goals of the Executive you support. You understand exactly what that person is expected to accomplish in every single moment of every single day, because you read those e-mails, because you track information, because you can anticipate where difficulties will arise. You are prepared and you almost welcome the element of unexpectedness. You manage the hassle-filled part of your role, and you do it with a smile and good humor (no matter how talented you are, your support system cannot be sustained unless you have a sense of humor behind it). And you can achieve this level of mastery because, as you and I know, what's going to happen will happen; what can go wrong, will go wrong. When we make a mistake – no, we don't dismiss it without accountability – we instead look at it and ask, "What have I learned?" By asking that question, you have just created a new response, a new opportunity for growth and success. It highlights your willingness to inform yourself for the future and strengthens your practice of making no assumptions. This is the essence of your strategy and is your most valuable contribution.

Initiative: Executive Assistants go beyond the call of duty, subordinating even personal self-interest to meet Executive expectations. The implications of your role are defined by intellectual prestige. Today's Executive Assistant embodies intellectual honesty and prestige. You are aware of the need to be resolute and steadfast to maintain your qualitative edge. You are constantly looking for ways to improve. You know that you need to understand global business principles, and to acquire experience in global communication, so that you can represent Executives in their dealings with clients. You are constantly engaged with, and seek out, new opportunities to learn and to demonstrate your newly acquired, essential skills.

Initiative, then, captures your ability to function with a level of "certainty." That is because you have secured within yourself and your experience an unchallenged level of skills. Moreover, you are constantly building upon those skills: Every time you bring a new idea to your computer, or to the Executive, you have just enhanced the viability of your career. In doing so, you have reliably confirmed that you are keeping up with, and applying, the pivotal components of your strategic support strategy, which include technological advancements. Keeping "current" with technology provides evidence of global social skills, practices and awareness that allow you to respond to different cultural and professional customs. It firmly proves you possess an open mind, one that encourages intellectual understanding of leadership and management skills (that are now components of the role). Above all, it paints your actions with the color of competence, inviting Executives to faithfully invest in the support you provide when taking the initiative.

Innovation: Innovation is the hunt for new value. One of the issues that I frequently discuss is how Executive Assistants encounter and manage different obstacles throughout the various stages of their careers, so they are inspired to introduce new support strategies, and they will always consider and pursue a new learning agenda. We know that new knowledge is essential. I stand in the space of "if we don't learn, we stay stagnant." And I am sure you will agree that ongoing learning is the appropriate response to the changes that we encounter. We know that today there are unexpected influences in our work; yet, we tend to disregard some of them. One such example is when we talk about global realization – it is more than a long-term idea; we must be able to connect its effect with what we do every single day.

Further, consider today's Executives who, in response to relentless global demand, may travel up to 80% of the time to stay competitive. What are you doing while they are traveling? I would like to think that you are exercising creative thinking, without hesitation, while processing and managing information; that you are making decisions on behalf of Executives because you are a supportive, Strategic Business Partner, and you have influenced yourself into that level of opportunity in order to manage the relentless and unexpected workflow.

Integrity: This fourth attribute is evidenced by trustworthiness, reliability, and accountability. Integrity discourages misunderstanding while encouraging open and honest communication and respectful listening. This is the component that creates superior value. Integrity – consistency of character – guides the decisions and activities of Executive Assistants when managing their responsibilities. Asking questions such as "What do I need to do so this oversight does not occur again?" instill an ethical reliability in your work that requires focus, authenticity, precision, judgment, and detail accuracy.

I have a great problem with anyone who sends me an e-mail with a typographical error. There is no reason for that! I do not care how fast you need to move. You need to stop, read your information, double-check your grammar. Be *absolutely* certain that there are no grammatical errors, because, let me tell you something: if you make a mistake in one thing, if you do not double-check your work, you will make a similar mistake in everything that you do. Double-checking e-mail grammar, reconfirming flight schedules, ensuring every detail related to meetings is accurate (purpose/agenda, list of attendees with biographical data that the Executive will need in order to know who is sitting at that table, even though he or she may already know), confirm your commitment to detail management.

Attention to detail supports what it is that you do, and directly affects how you are perceived. Indeed, Executive Assistants' competitive advantage is the ability to recognize the need to take more time to reflect on what is most important in order to create ways to overcome challenges. We need to find ways to sort through myriad demands and distractions. Fact-checking to enable focus and clarity is among the Executive Assistant's most important competence.

An additional critical aspect of integrity is judgment, which underscores the strength of character. You do not speak negatively about the person with whom you work. You do not share information because there is an expected confidentiality in everything that you do, and for self-protection, you do not participate in the "gossip stream." So, the reality is that Executive Assistants today assume a professional stance, and by that, I mean "Executive-like" behavior. You guide conversations that take place every moment, speaking to everyone with great respect, honoring each person's presence. Even though you may be busy, there is a way to say "no." There is a way to say, "not now" with great respect and with a smile. And, saying "no" and making someone feel good about your having said "no" – that is a very special talent. It is a level of political achievement that most people cannot capture. But the masterful individuals who support Executives can do that. Because, as you know, these reliable contributors are indeed the "fixers".

These four "I's", Intuition, Initiative, Innovation and Integrity, comprise the premise and support the main attributes of intellectual recognition. These remain the non-negotiable essential skills and characteristics of the Professional Executive Assistant.

When I served as an Executive Assistant, the prevalent view of strategic reliability responded to the concept of 24/7/365. I was always expected to be available. Let me tell you, when I did this work, I did not have a life! That was the bottom line. Now, that doesn't mean I didn't have fun time, family time, time for myself; that is not what I am suggesting. But I am suggesting that you are reliable and accessible to that person you support, or to that team that you support. So that cell phone, or that iPad, or that laptop, is always engaged, no matter where you are or what you are doing. You are constantly aware that you will be called upon at some point, at some time, in the evening, on the weekend – yes, on a Sunday morning, to help to solve a problem. That is what the purpose of this role was, and to good measure, remains.

Co-author Loretta Sophocleous, thankfully, shares an updated standard for us to consider. She tells us that strategic responsibility responds to the concept of 24/7/365 availability; however, no one can *always* be available. Therefore, we must ensure that our teams are aware of our ongoing projects and that there is clarity on their evolution. In addition, we should always have a back-up plan in place. For instance, during vacation and personal travel you can commit to putting in an hour or so every day to check on relevant emails. I always advise my staff that if something needs my immediate attention, they should highlight the word "critical" in the subject line. In addition, I am always available to them by cell phone. This position requires prudent responsibility, but it should not preclude one from having a life. In support of that reality, studies have shown that not taking time for yourself is counter-productive to both you and the enterprise.

You are a problem-solver. You are a strategist. You know how to get someone from Point A to Point B, and not lose them. What is necessary, however, is the skill of time allocation. Know what you need to do; know what is required, then allocate time for your personal life management.

If you work with someone who allows you access to their e-mail, that is one standard which enables you to read through, assess, prioritize, and know exactly what you need to do to bring the day forward. If you work with someone who does not allow you access to his or her e-mail (and there are some Executives who do not), then it is up to you to find out from that Executive what is vital, critical, and what must happen every day. That is your responsibility, not theirs; if you miss that person, pick up the phone or send a text and find out what needs to be done.

You are never losing. You are moving on a path that takes you directly to success. And that success has its influence throughout your organization. Those Assistants who do not yet understand the influence capacity that you represent or the skillsets that you bring, those who do not know how to manage appropriately on a day-to-day basis, have not yet reached this high-performance level.

The other imperative is to acquire a keen sense of how to manage the expectations of the Executive you support. To me, the key aspect of achieving this goal is determined by the Executive/Executive Assistant Business Partnership relationship, which is the gateway to success. It is within this context that I remind you to never – and I mean never – work for someone you neither trust, nor respect. You will not realize your greatness, nor will you experience the gratification that is the outcome of a reliable business relationship. The personality match is the most significant and reliable aspect of this role's success. You must have a high regard for the Executive with whom you work. Why? Because this role is about Executive Life Management, and you care about and want the best for that person. With personality match, trust and respect, you will achieve victories that you could not imagine. You always will be running on a fast track, and you will perform beyond expectations.

If you neither like nor respect the Executive you support, it is unlikely that you will go outside of the boundaries of your role to help that individual to be successful. That's just human nature. So, do not sell yourself short by accepting undesirable circumstances, or working with someone who does not have a high regard for what you do every single day to ensure successful outcomes for that individual. Respect is the ultimate currency.

There is a time, I think, in everyone's life when you take a moment to sit back and ask, "Why am I doing what I am doing every single day?" I know what it is that I do, and I can learn to do it better. The question is: why? And that is something that we all need to understand, especially when you are managing the undefined support role that helps others to be great, while you are encountering so many circumstances for things to go awry.

So, what is it that inspires you to achieve and meet challenges every single day - from going into that office, sitting down at that desk, and finding the totally unexpected problems that you did not think you would encounter the night before when you left? What is it that you achieve from that experience? The answer to these questions will inform you as to whether or not you are in the right role. If you do not realize any satisfaction whatsoever, rather, you experience frustration, distraction, or upset, then you may want to rethink why you do this work.

But if you gain satisfaction from even the least of what you have achieved with no acknowledgement expected (because that acknowledgement is rare), if you gain satisfaction from being able to be ahead of the problem, which is what this role is, then you fit! This is for you. Now, let's look at what it is that you do, and why.

First, you provide Strategic Support. This means that you are watching every single moment of every single day, exercising your Executive-like capacity to determine where problems might be, while helping the Executive to better plan his or her day. I have known of Executives who arrange meetings on their calendars without looking at what may already exist. Now, you come in the next morning and every time slot is booked; everyone has put something on that calendar. Your role is to look and say, "This does not make any sense. I am going to take x, y and z off that calendar. I am going to move those people to maybe the next day, or maybe the next week." How are you able to do that? Because you know what is important to that Executive. You also know that the Executive tends to do this all the time. Why, because he or she can't ever say "no." And because you know that person always says "yes" to everything, you need to be checking that calendar. And you need to make sure that your "yes" to everything is appropriate.

Suppose the Executive comes out and says: "Why did you take Melba off the calendar?" Your response? "Well, you are seeing Melba next Thursday at a dinner, I have positioned you right beside her at that dinner, so you can have your conversation then. With that change on your calendar, you now have an hour to have lunch." Managing in this style and manner confirms caring for the person, which is knowing what is important in that person's life. That is also making sure that nothing gets lost in the translation; that nothing gets put aside that is not accounted for. This is your "why."

Executive Assistants today often work from master lists. I see lists and lists and lists...but you know what I often do not see? I don't see dates for accountability. I don't see completion dates. So, I can have 50 items on my to-do list, and unless I sit there and really identify the absolute date of completion for every single item, and share that with the Executive I support, so that we are working together in partnership on the same activity list, what I have is a list of conversations that can go nowhere, mean nothing, or get "lost in the cracks." Dates for accountability make to-do lists essential, and the Executive or the team you support must be a part of those decisions in terms of the prioritization of activities. There is no way around that. And to suggest that "you didn't tell me" or "I didn't know" – those are not conversations that a top-level Executive Assistant ever wants to have. Nor should you. There is opportunity all the time to get the information that you need.

Second, *you provide Leadership*. Leadership is often qualified as having others follow you, but that is only a surface glance. I am not talking about that level of leadership. Rather, Executive Assistants understand that as Leaders, character is their #1 attribute. This distinguishing characteristic confirms how you cope with change, push through obstacles to finish what you start, handle difficulties and emergencies. Confirms the distinction you demonstrate in how you present yourself, how you speak, how you dress. Confirms the way in which you communicate with others, such as offering solutions to problems - not because you want to be the star of the moment, but because you want to help others, because you think that what you know can help them to be a little better at what they do. That is Leadership. It is how you bring others along. And it receives no recognition. Why? Because it is a natural outcome of – first of all – liking yourself. Secondly, it manifests as you learn more about what needs to be done, in the world and at your desk (which *is* the world...yes, the world is at your desk, all the time), and as you inspire others to be successful. That is Executive Assistant Leadership.

Third, you provide Management. As Managers, you direct individuals and routines through organizational adaptability. You are inventive, resilient, resourceful. And you anticipate – anticipation is where you excel. For example, you know there is a series of meetings taking place: Who is attending those meetings? What is the agenda? Do we have all of the supporting documents, and have those details been double-checked? Triple-checked? Is the information accurate? Is everyone reminded the day before that there is a meeting the next morning? Your mind moves to answer these questions even before they are asked.

Managing these answers is your responsibility, not the Assistants who work for the other guests, it is yours – because I am assuming that you are working for, let's say, the senior person, which means that everything that takes place in that person's life becomes your responsibility. Integral to this process is implementation or solving for success. You identify the problem, gather the relevant data, test possible solutions, and proceed to the goal. So, accountability for every detail, making sure everything is in order for that Executive, is your imperative. It is the hallmark of your position.

Those who understand Strategic Support, Leadership and Management, know how these skills are recognized and applauded at the Executive Assistant level. These practices build a strong brand, and are reflected in the strategies of Intuition, Initiative, Innovation and Integrity.

Do not in any way underestimate your value, or the caliber of what it is that you bring every single day. Do not for one moment think that technology has displaced you. You are always aware that your capabilities are augmented by digital technologies, which drives operating efficiency at the Executive Assistant level. We benefit from technologies that force us to rethink how to respond to real-time information systems; thus, expanding our ability to make informed decisions with greater efficiency. This does not deprive us of our brain power.

Technology, as magical as it is, has encouraged us to think beyond what is on the screen. The computer does not ask questions; it answers them. The computer does not tell you that the Executive is 15 minutes late in getting to the next meeting; that is for you to track. Computers are tools - the best computer user understands that. Your task is to find out as much information as you can. Research has become a tremendous component of what you do, but common-sense overrides research. What would you want and need to know if you were that CEO in the focus? You do not expect a computer to spew out that information because it simply cannot. So, let us not participate in conversations about computers replacing Executive Assistants. It is unlikely to happen, and only at the expense of corporate business effectiveness.

Why? Because intelligence and innovative skills are the human components that allow Executive Assistants to automatically think through what is required to meet Executive expectation. And there is something else that computers do not yet have: the skill of empathy. Empathy means that you can observe someone in distress. Empathy means that you step away from someone's behavior, and we know that sometimes Executives demonstrate a behavior that is not necessarily what we would like to be encountering at the moment. It allows you to see what is happening, especially if you know what is taking place in this Executive's life. It has nothing to do with you. The minute you insert yourself into that conversation, it is about your ego. Not about the circumstances.

Empathy allows us to see the circumstances. It allows us to be gracious to others, even though we may not want to at the moment, because we can see what that person needs. This is a huge quality - a huge skill - for Executive Assistants! The skill of empathy is a social skill. It enables you to step through circumstances without making them your own. It enables you to not judge other people's behavior; it enables you to see through the problem toward the creative solution, with kindness and compassion.

Professional Executive Assistants are applauded for their ability to develop operational strategies that include policies, procedures, technology solutions and network integration. They are recognized for organizing a strategy around execution and new learning to maximize efficiency. And all while they manage their relationships with the skill of empathy.

If you have stepped into a manager/subordinate relationship, that we have been culturally conditioned to accept, know that such a role is archaic. That hypothesis should no longer exist, least of all in your mind. You are "Business Partners." Why? Because you both have the same objective and attitude about success. Because you each have the same goal, which is "let's get it done and let's get it done right." You each have the same competitive sense of well-being because when you win, it is a great feeling; when you lose, there is a chance to learn something – for both of you.

So, let's think about what the commitment is to this role. Let's think about the responsibility that you have when you take on this level of support. Because with Leadership, Management, and Strategic Support, you are now a Business Partner! You are not subservient. You are a partner; in line with the Executive you see every day, or not. You are a partner. And thinking as a partner means that the company's success and the Executive's success is the essential purpose of your role. It means that everything you do connects to your influential impact on the success of both.

There is no greater career, in my opinion, than that of the Executive Assistant. It draws upon all your talents, all your temperament sources. It draws upon everything you are able to do. And, ultimately, the role is about helping someone else, or a team, or your company, to be successful. There is a level of achievement that may not always be acknowledged but always will be recognized.

My preoccupation with the title of global Executive Life Mana is that Assistants need to understand economic influences; you need to understand marketing, Executive leadership, global interference. Imperative is your ability to learn and respond with appropriate, global communication skills. You know that we are no longer running on a track of repetitiveness, doing the same things over and again.

No. We are realizing how unexpected influences come to us, how they have a bearing on what it is that we do every single day, while we are appropriately managing ourselves and those around us.

More on Intuition, Initiative, Innovation, and Integrity

In deeper reflection, I am reiterating that the common denominators for Executive Assistant support strategy are Intuition, Initiative, Innovation, and Integrity. To that formula, I add Insight. Insight has been described as the joining together of two or more pieces of information or data in a unique way to arrive at a new approach, service or solution that delivers value, and connects the dots in new and creative ways. Integrity discourages misunderstanding while it encourages open and honest communication and respectful listening. Together, four practices— Intuition, Initiative, Innovation, and Integrity— configure our Insight and ability to deliver value.

With increasing competitive pressures, the pace of change keeps accelerating as companies search for even higher levels of quality, service, and overall business agility. To survive in this environment, we must learn to be comfortable on the edge, for that is where exploration, growth, self-mastery, maturity, and profits are found. From that cutting edge, we will be better able to develop transformable ways of managing our lives and our careers. Albert Einstein tells us that "the measure of intelligence is the ability to change."

Old ideas are our biggest liability, simply because while that idea or way of being was an asset yesterday,

yesterday is gone. You can do things the same way for years, look around one day, and find yourself out of step with the speed of business. And that is neither good nor bad; it is, simply, expected. How do *you* innovate?

Let me leave you with this idea: Once a standard has achieved critical mass, its value to everyone multiplies exponentially. So, accept that global Executive Assistants have a constantly changing position description that requires building upon your skills to achieve and maintain your professional status. As with every profession, ongoing education remains necessary. Steve Jobs tells us "Do what you love. View setbacks as opportunities. Dedicate yourself to the passionate pursuit of excellence."

Remember that NO is a complete sentence. Remember that honest self-assessment is a good character skill. Remember that Emotional Intelligence is realized by the patience to learn, and a willingness to try new ideas.

Sixty-Second Leadership©

Be Self-Aware. Name what is present. Increase your ability to feel what you are feeling when you are feeling it by naming it, without judgment: "I am bored." "I am angry." "I am afraid."

Observe. Take a step back, psychologically; observe your state of being. You will always enhance your sense of proportion about an experience, even if only slightly, by stepping out of that experience and looking at it.

CHAPTER II

Are Executive Assistants
A Dying Breed?

I was recently interviewed for a *Washington Post* article ("Administrative Assistant Jobs Helped Propel Many Women into the Middle Class. Now They're Disappearing", December 4, 2019). I am always surprised by this persisting perception because there has been verifiable and acknowledged shifts in the functional role of the Executive Assistant from support to management to leadership. Now, please take note. This ever-evolving role creates superb results for Executives and their companies. It is the very nature of the fluidity and ever-demanding call to new skills mastery, I believe, that has some lament the irrelevance of the profession's "traditional" functions. More so here than in many professions, yesterday's solutions are often ineffective today. I am reminded of this by American humorist Mark Twain's often misquoted quip on the report of his death: "The reports of my death are greatly exaggerated."

Let's get right to it. Rapid technological change, global integration of the U.S. economy and generational distinctions directly impact today's workforce. Executives and Assistants are wrestling with the following key questions: How do I keep pace with the rate of innovation in the new economic environment? What is the right balance of new skills? Am I able to keep up with the superior capabilities being demanded by business? How do I create value? What is the purpose and role of the Executive Assistant?

This is a timely topic, because generationally this role has changed. Yet, we still sometimes hear that the Executive Assistant is a dying breed. That software and office automation are quickly making the position obsolete. That Executives simply do not need that kind of person-to-person help anymore.

The assisting position is inherently difficult and becoming more so. Consider the following: new demands are placed upon those who drive the mission of their business; thus, new demands are also placed upon those who support them in their efforts. I am seeing an emerging consensus that these forces make possible the unprecedented expansion for extraordinarily talented and incredibly hardworking Executive Assistants.

So why are some still unenthused about this profession? Well, this is not a sustainable role unless you change the trajectory. This is a major undertaking. The reality is that in our 21st century business world, the most valued attribute is a demonstrated willingness to understand and to embrace change. Let's consider some of the major changes Executive Assistants have had to endure: First, the invention of revolutionary new technologies; second, economic expansion and contractions; third, demographic shifts; and fourth, expanding markets.

Executive Assistants have benefited because these challenges have promoted upward mobility in the position. Meeting these changes require Assistants to create knowledge and tools that are useful and, yes, transferable. The metamorphosis is evident. The signs are clear. Executive Assistants have effectively emerged from the tradition of "doing what they are told to do" to a new level of mastery, which is "doing what needs to be done, when and how it needs to be done," with confidence.

Still, the profession remains haunted by examples of exemplary work that fails to be properly compensated. This, from Loretta Sophocleous: "Many, many years ago when I worked for a well-known Fortune 500 company, before the term 'Executive Assistant' referred to our present-day profession, there was a class of Executives who were, at that time, known as 'Executive Assistants'. They reported directly to the CEO and President of the company. They were at that time (many, many years ago) already earning a salary in the six figures. The position was a progression for them to move into a high-level management spot at the C-Suite level."

"When these Executive Assistants reached that level, there was a vacancy that needed to be filled. While looking for the next person to fill the vacancy, the CEO/President asked their 'secretary' if they could temporarily fill in. What happened next should not surprise any of us. The secretary carried out the functions so flawlessly along with their normal duties that eventually they no longer needed the very coveted position of Executive Assistant, as it was then known. Unfortunately, the secretary's efforts were never openly acknowledged nor were they appropriately compensated for the extra work."

Now there is a fierce urgency for precise techniques, the meticulous pursuit of efficiency, and appropriate compensation. These are today's inescapable requirements.

Executive Assistants haven't been phased out; they are now essential. The new Executive Assistant, or Executive Life Manager, grasps the concept of change, applies creativity and innovation to their everyday process, and is now trusted with even more bottom-line accountability.

Keeping up with the changes in office automation has, if anything, made them more essential than ever. Freed from the routine tasks of the past, Executive Assistants are the people who keep our offices, and our economy, humming with unmatched regularity. Many of these consummate team players keep Executives' lives manageable by their skills in expectations management, and by seamlessly interweaving the varied details of business and personal agendas.

Executive Assistants expect to learn continuously and focus on how to make existing processes work better. In an economy driven by ideas and intellectual know-how, employers seek out and retain those employees who are smart, have relevant skills and are highly creative; new ideas are welcomed, and input is sought in solving problems. A great opportunity occurs for the Executive Assistant, because connecting process innovation to the role means not waiting for someone to tell you how to do your job better. Innovation is more than the creative application of acquired skills; innovation facilitates the discovery of new avenues of improvement and capabilities. Consider the advice of the esteemed author and management consultant, Peter F. Drucker, in his book, *Essential Drucker*: "There is surely nothing quite so useless as doing with great efficiency what should not be done at all." Executive Assistants can boast an almost unprecedented reputation as rigorous masters of change and synchronization.

These tasks are a good deal more delicate than simply punching off items on a to-do-list. Microsoft will never develop software that can adeptly manage critical business processes, and within a single hour, calm a hysterical sales manager, send a birthday card to a manager's grandchild, avert a crisis by redrafting a poorly-worded email, keep track of flights on take-off and landing, confirm that Executive transportation is waiting in the right place at the right time, soothe a ruffled caller, and arrange for flowers to be sent to a recently bereaved employee. These Executive Assistants save Executives' time and stress, give their companies a human face, and always will be essential!

If well-suited to the role, the experienced Executive Assistant will recognize and be empowered by the "fit" with the Executive, and the relationship between that commitment and job satisfaction. My conversations with senior Executives confirm that they now rely more than ever on their "right-and-left-hand-person."

In today's business environment, more and more, the Executive Assistant plays a critical role in helping senior Executives achieve their company's goals. They provide a "safety net" by supporting Executives in the integration of all elements of management plans so that implementation is fluid and seamless.

I am reminded that in my career as an Executive Assistant, I had to learn to listen, understand, influence; to persuade, negotiate with, sell or present an idea to; to deliver bad news and good news. Experience taught me that timing, or reading the moment, was one of the most important skills that I had to master. That was the key to being successful in getting things done. I learned that processes, procedures, goals, and objectives were essential to maintaining priorities; and that with "messaging skills" there had to be substance. Having fallen into these traps myself, one lesson remains with me to this day: Blame has no space in the delivery of excellent performance. There are no excuses. Rather, focus on what is wrong that must be immediately solved, and how to do it, rather than who did it wrong, when it was done wrong and why someone else did it wrong.

What does it take to be great? Understanding strategy. Peter Drucker reminds us that "efficiency is doing the thing right; effectiveness is doing the right thing." Executive Assistants possess the experience of knowing how to do things well, knowing which things should be done in the first place, and which should not. This calls for the ability to manage the present and the future at the same time. Herein lies the opportunity for greater expansion within the role. Here's what a client of ours tells us about these unique skills:

"An exemplary Executive Assistant is technology proficient, has common sense and has superb judgment.

By that I mean that he/she exercises the ability to diagnose a situation, does not reveal information that should remain in confidence, has a sophisticated understanding of boundaries in different situational contexts, does not act outside of established procedures and policies, and does not argue a point of view." This strategy represents broad knowledge and perspective, mental fitness, and experience. With these success skills, Executive Assistants' strategic advantage is gained through ingenuity and in their ability to prepare for and respond to unpredictable events; they exercise their "clairvoyance" skills.

Setting goals is the indispensable key to the reason high achievers accomplish so much. And the people who most frequently reach their goals are those who write them down and develop plans and deadline dates to accomplish them. Remember *Alice in Wonderland*? At one point in the story, Alice stops at a crossroad to ask the Cheshire Cat which road to take. He responds by asking where she wants to go. When she tells him she "doesn't much care where," he replies, "then, it doesn't much matter which way you go." To set a goal is to chart a road map to success.

Here are ways to structure processes, procedures, goals and objectives into your everyday practice: Focus on *What*, not Who; on *Now*, not When; on *We*, not They; on *How*, not Why. I have also learned to give up "certainty," and that making assumptions are deadly.

And so, let me to introduce you to the Executive Assistant who knows that the key is to match personality to circumstance. Meet the individual who is secure, self-confident, is in control of his/her attitude, is continuously improving, learning, and applying new skills. One who is honest, tactful, and exercises good judgment. A person who is publicly modest, who thinks before speaking, and who manages confidentiality.

This is your tenacious support individual, who is committed to the result, regardless of what has to be endured along the way. This is the person who learns something new every day, improves in technical expertise, and manages relationships with awareness, common sense and honesty.

The people in the ranks of top management have always had a list of things they can't do without help from a real, live human being – someone who knows virtually everything of consequence about the Executive and the company for which he or she works. I would argue that this list is typically longer today than it was even last year, and that the Executive Assistant who helps to manage this list is now one of the most important players in the entire organization.

For a successful, collegial working relationship to develop, mutual expectations must be established through open and respectful communication. A solid relationship is not based on a stand-off perspective. I am reminded of the telegram from a theatrical producer to playwright George Bernard Shaw: *"Send manuscript. If good, will send check."* Shaw replied: *"Send check. If good, will send manuscript."* You know there has to be adaptability, which is the art of creating appropriate solutions to respond to the circumstances that will arise.

When you think about it, this role is more difficult now.In recent years, with all these skills, professional

Executive Assistants have, in fact, become a sub-layer of management itself, and are more, not less, indispensable. Today, they manage carefully-engineered schedules and time-critical contingency plans; they exercise a form of leadership and management within their companies that is less visible than traditional forms, yet more significant; they keep pace with Executives who travel extensively; and they keep up with changing technology and information overload, which requires a good filtering strategy. Their sustainable advantage is in their ability to manage these four heavily demanding (but indispensable!) skills, which are among the key aspects of the role.

Executive Assistants are champions of the workplace. Those who are inclined toward this profession discover that its inherent complexities and challenges produce immense satisfaction, and a sense of contribution and accomplishment. Executive Assistants draw from all their talents, intelligence, developed intuition, common sense skill and positive attitudes in their pursuit of professional excellence. The talented, experienced Executive Assistant is among the most sought-after level of hire today. Busy Executives are desperate for quality, focused, experienced support in all areas of their lives.

The Executive Assistant always will function as the essential point person upon which the constant challenge and success of effective Executive work management will revolve. This career is here to stay.

Sixty-Second Leadership©

Social-Awareness: Project positive intent. Most people do not go to work saying, "I am going to be really mean today!" Their behavior and intention, from their point of view, is positive or productive. We are all doing the best we can and, sometimes, we fail. When you are listening to someone, consider from the point of view that they want to achieve something positive even if their behavior is off-putting. You will project some intent, why not imagine something positive? There is no additional charge for this option.

CHAPTER III

What Is Your Differentiator?

Let's first imagine for one second that you are carrying a briefcase, stuffed with all the things you have in your working life. Now, imagine that I am offering to lend you a hand to help you to empty your briefcase, and that you are going to allow me to help you to refill it. You agree. However, there is one caveat: if self-interest is your hidden motive, this will be a hindrance and a burden to you and will impede our progress. Not every feeling that seems good is at once to be acted upon, nor is every feeling that runs contrary to our inclinations to be immediately rejected. You need do just one thing: as I present practices for you to place in your briefcase, you must make a mental note of which current practices you would like to remove.

Are you easily distracted? Are you easily upset by the opposition of others? What is the opportunity cost? This is your golden opportunity to self-assess and to find your place to stand. Understanding what you are uniquely qualified to bring to the assisting position and what you are incapable of bringing to it, is a courageous footing from which to face up to what motivates you, and what skills you may need to refresh or acquire. Now, let's fill the briefcase with a sense of purpose.

Assistants: What kind of impact do you want to have this year and for the future? I respond to that question by confirming traditional foundation skills, which emphasize the attributes and skills that, in my experience, remain the most important for an Executive Assistant.

Traditional skills:

- Social and interpersonal – maintain positive relationships; practice discretion and good judgment; be open-minded to, and accepting of, criticism.
- Grammar, writing, and proofreading.
- Confirm details.
- Mental, verbal, and numerical ability.
- Critical problem-solving skills – analyze, prioritize, take initiative and solve problems; above all, work in a focused state, with undivided attention.

Possession of the traditional skillset aids in your ability to navigate through complexity, to establish priorities, plan and organize: You are assertive, tough-minded, and tactful. You manage deadlines while maintaining close attention to detail. You prepare for the opposite of what you expect, just in case.

Most important, you are in control of your attitude. Self-confidence, self-management, self-discipline, and self-awareness are your strengths. With continuous improvement of processes as the appropriate goal, you are an enthusiastic learner and an essential support system for Executives. You know that decision-making is the absorption of uncertainty, and that "doing" produces learning. Your outlook and approach turn obstacles into opportunities, making no goal seem impossible.

Have you heard anything yet that you would like to add to that briefcase? Now, let me introduce the formula for the imperative self-sustaining skills required for today's successful Executive Assistant: Management + Leadership + Strategic Support = Business Partnership.

Management: This is a matter of constantly looking at the way you do things and accessing your resources to adjust the process to reflect Executives' goals. With scheduling power, you help Executives to more effectively manage their day. As managers, Executive Assistants take an idea from conception to research, analysis, collaboration, team building, execution, and follow-through. *Key skills: high level of Sophistication in Communications, Interpersonal Relations, and Diplomacy.*

Leadership: This is your ability to motivate and inspire others to respond positively to change; to demonstrate your self-sustaining skills strategy and to thereby communicate with positive energy the new relevance of this profession. With your intelligence, and skills of observation and awareness, you confirm that continuous improvement of processes is the appropriate goal. You are the eyes and ears of the Executive; you function in the role of Ambassador for the Executive, while you buffer communication with others. *Key skills: Integrity, Selflessness, Emotional Stability and Resilience.*

Strategic Support: This is your ability to solve problems – exercise good judgment; look inward and identify ways that may inadvertently contribute to the organization's problems; with confidence, suggest changes in strategy. *Key skills: Time Allocation, Prioritization, Troubleshooting.* Most important is *Keen Judgment*:

- Know when to speak, and when to remain silent.
- Know what information is reliable and what needs to be questioned and challenged.
- Know how to create and manage a reporting system that allows for task management and follow-up to completion.
- Know how to respond to unanticipated developments; how to best keep the Executive focused on the top priorities.

Management + Leadership + Strategic Support = Business Partnership. This is the modern Architecture of the Support Role. The burden of change rests not just with a few people, but with people at every level, and especially at the key Administrative Support level. Only when companies endorse the work of the Executive Assistant as Leader, Manager, Support Specialist, and Business Partner will this move forward.

What is Your Differentiator?

You must be empathetically programmed for this role. And you must have the ability to recognize the potential of the position: focus on long-term priorities and opportunities, inspire others, and reinforce critical organizational values. You are intelligent, trustworthy, and admired. Purpose, Accountability and Competence combined – that is your Differentiator.

An Assistant's special role is to make the life of the Executive easier; to keep the Executive informed and abreast of situations s/he would not focus on while doing his/her job. Most relevant is the ability of the Assistant to understand the personal and business context of the Executive, within which he/she must manage the day-to-day responsibilities of the role. Doing so requires the following:

- The imperative of "fit" – with respect to environment, personality, work content, work habits and appropriate compensation.

- Improving one's listening skills – acquire a keen sense of where problems are most likely to be and with whom. Be a trouble-shooter: when you run into a problem, try to think of at least two solutions before you take that problem to the Executive.

- Helping the Executive to make consistent decisions by advising the Executive of historical (not hysterical) and/or evolving precedents.

- Improving quality results by studying, evaluating, and re-designing processes.

- Demonstrating preparedness with the ability to answer the questions you know you will be asked.

And remember, this is a Business Partnership. Executives must contribute in equal ways to ensure its success. To do so, an Executive must:

- Improve his/her listening skills.

- Be clear about the responsibilities of the role (business, personal/family) – full disclosure, no surprises, or unstated expectations.

- Provide crystal clear communication on all matters.
- Provide opportunities for new learning and advancement within the role.
- Avoid control talk: "What can I do to make your job easier?" vs. "I don't understand why..."
- Share relevant information that would affect your decision-making or process.

With these guidelines in mind, let us examine how Purpose, Accountability, and Competence ensure not only success, but excellence in this endeavor.

Purpose: Purpose is found in your ability to build this strategic partnership. Not every Executive/Executive Assistant team gets to choose their Assistant or Executive; therefore, every partnership will have a different experience. But as a skilled Assistant, you can create a good working relationship if you have a tactic and a strategy. Your purpose is to ensure that your effectiveness will optimize the performance of the Executive you support. Assistants create the new paradigm: speed (the ability to make effective decisions quickly) and determination to excel (singular commitment to a chosen purpose) are your core strengths.

Accountability: You know that the rapid changes in business have created pressure for enhanced productivity. These changes mean added responsibility, shortened response times, the need for close collaboration both within and without the immediate organization (often during stressful times of change), heightened sensitivity to cross-cultural differences, and generally, more knowledge of business and industry. *But you are Masters of Change.* You surpass all expectations in performance and levels of efficiency, despite this bewildering "change environment." No longer will your performance be measured by the implication of your role, but rather by your ability to change, and by your individual contribution.

Competence: As previously stated, Assistants are expected to survive in this changing environment by being comfortable on the "edge" where exploration, growth, self-mastery, and self-achievement are born. Surviving on that cutting-edge means developing transformable ways of managing our lives and our careers.

The Executive Assistant possesses significant influence and drives this change. You are recognized as a lynchpin in any organization. No one will argue with the premise that inadequate administrative support and inadequately skilled teams can derail even the most successful companies. Assistants, you hold together the systems, procedures and policies; you represent the values of your organization. You contribute to the well-being of your organization. You play a critical role in day-to-day issues. You know the importance of managing all levels of detail.

A key aspect of your role is to act as sounding boards and provide feedback, in many cases before policy is finalized. Today, an "Executive decision" may be, at least in part, an Executive Assistant decision, as well. Your expertise in up-to-date software applications will ensure that all work is timely and accurate. To survive in this environment, it is your responsibility to keep abreast of technology's ever-quickening pace, so that you may continue to provide innovation, information and support. You adopt and demonstrate the guiding principles of influence:

- The art of discernment
- Prudence
- Integrity
- Reliability
- Emotional and intellectual maturity
- Self-confidence

How is that briefcase looking now?

What will make you stand out above the rest? You know that:

- You are always individually, by choice, able to take control of creating and managing an impressive professional image.
- You are expected to adapt to the changes in a dynamic global business environment.
- You benefit from diversity by valuing differences.
- Learning and improvement are key.
- Lifelong learning means building on strengths.

You work tirelessly to cultivate specific talents: energy, drive, creativity, and the ability to work effectively with others. And to be clear, "effectively" means towards a common goal with respect and trust and in as simple and straightforward a way as possible. It is common sense and respect for the integrity of others that will keep us from engaging in this work lightly or carelessly.

You know that anything is possible with the right skills, the right attitude, and a thorough understanding of the role you play in your organization and how what you do impacts others. Being "street smart"/adaptive while being creative are strong motivators, and motivation drives us to succeed.

You confirm that technology, as an idea, is how compatibility of previously incompatible parts creates a new whole. At any moment, we can see things in totality. What this means is that as machines master information, Assistants are relied upon for their "conceptual skills, "imagination" and "innovation."

You are an expert tightrope walker. This is quite a skill to be mastered, especially as you are not alone up there on that high wire – although it may feel that way sometimes. One misstep – a hasty decision, an e-mail that was not worded properly, not proofread carefully, a clash with a co-worker – and you or somebody else may come tumbling off that high wire. Yes, it is really quite a balancing act. To keep yourself and others safe on that wire, you must understand how everything that you do is inextricably linked to everyone else.

You know what kind of job you want and why. You study the Executive's personality, style, and preferences; you know the best time and the best manner in which to present information; as a rule: you always look at decisions made from the Executive's point of view; exercise "soft power": you do not try to change the Executive; rather, where appropriate, you suggest scenarios that may not have been considered as an complementary point of view;

you prepare the Executive for the possibility of an alternate reaction to his/her decision, thus enabling him/her to be confident in responding to this eventuality.

You make no assumptions: you do not assume that you know the Executive's goals. To that end, you make sure that you are fully aware of what the Executive is trying to accomplish. You ask clarifying questions and point out inconsistencies when tasks seem out of line with stated goals. You ensure that priorities are in line with those of the Executive.

You are willing to create the partnership suggestions, showcase your flexibility and understanding and remember to consider the decision from the Executive's point of view.

Purpose, Accountability and Competence Is Your Differentiator

The most important thing in communication, says management guru, Peter Drucker, is "to hear what isn't being said." In your efforts to alleviate some of the demands your Executive faces, you undoubtedly find yourself balancing what you know with what you have come to understand and anticipate; what has been stated with what has actually been asked; what is expected with what is needed. This is no small feat, and it is by no means accidental. It occurs because this position makes you *aware*; the importance of this distinction cannot be overstated. Good communication is critical in the workplace. It is listening without judgment (to distinguish what isn't being said) that allows you to focus and concentrate on specified tasks that confirm the conditions for your success. You pull things together, keep them together and make things happen! "Time is an illusion, lunch time doubly so," says Douglas Adams. What should be done, must be done – always. Executive Assistants must love the role and the partnership "fit" in spite of its unreasonable demands. You are the key communications node for the informal, and by far the most effective, communications network. It is for the Executive to remember William Shakespeare: "I can no other answer make, but, thanks, and thanks."

Admittedly, it is more difficult today for an Assistant to know what is happening with her or his Executive because Executives handle many things on their own. Many Executives do not allow their Assistant to manage their e-mails, leaving the Assistant in the dark and unable to be proactive or prepare for the unexpected. What then?

We could all be more productive if we did only what we are gifted to do; if we utilized those skills that we most enjoy, that we are good at, and if we siphoned off to someone we trust those tasks that we do less well – those that annoy, debilitate, distract and deter us from achieving our goals. Smart Executives realize that they need to replicate themselves, harness their worst tendencies and find someone to support them who has as fully-committed a sense of the business as they do. Most Senior Executives now rely more than ever on their "Professional Executive Assistant", who fills the roles of advance person and right-hand person. The success of an Assistant is in part related to the Executive's ability to trust, delegate and communicate clearly; achieving success becomes more difficult if those elements are lacking.

Yet, Executive Assistants know how to glean information from the Executive; how to obtain the answers you need without constantly interrupting or interrogating the Executive. You know how to listen for what hasn't been said, and you are in the position to act on that information. This requires that you build trust as a collaborator. State what you are going to do and meet expectations that are set. Being aware and attentive allows you to ask the right questions and shape the right strategy.

You must learn and know when to be proactive, and when to refrain and exercise the interpersonal competence to finesse difficult situations and people. You must know how to place facts in context and deliver them with impact. You must be a collaborator; and you must accept responsibility for your mistakes. Learn how to be an ally even under the most difficult circumstances.

Executive Assistants possessing such indispensable traits, capabilities, and diversity of talent represent a major segment of the talent pool in a highly competitive marketplace that companies simply cannot afford to ignore. This offers compelling advantages and opens up to Executive Assistants a world of infinite possibilities.

The effective organization recognizes that the competencies Executive Assistants need are changing dramatically. Professional Executive Assistants work confidentially with Executives, are expected to be open to new ideas, and to turn insights into new skills in order to keep pace with business leaders. Executive Assistants contribute at the highest levels to environments where markets are highly networked, organizations are global and information technology suffuses everything a company does. The Assistant's contribution is in the ability to handle work that is fast paced, requiring an extraordinary number of skills that are displayed in quick motion. Processing information, making decisions quickly, grouping tasks, and making intuitive judgments on the fly are manifestations of intelligence, awareness and adaptability to change. Competence reigns: it turns a strategy into an operating system from which to execute.

As Executives face the growing pressures of competitiveness, they will of necessity drive creativity and innovation at the Executive Assistant level by granting decision-making power and authority to take action to those Assistants who view change as an opportunity; to those who provide a source of new ideas, who function interdependently and who manage communication that is face-to-face, by phone or e-mail; to those who demonstrate that they know most about a task, and who are truly committed to their employer's success.

The very concrete aspects of the role of the Executive Assistant are familiar. What is needed is an Exhilarating Vision. One that will capture the hopes, goals and direction for the future of this role, and publicly declare the new and differentiating capabilities for building global mindset thinking and skills in your organizations. This vision will embrace change as an opportunity and provide the focus and energy to create an expanding universe for this position. It will be a powerful message to Executives, who earnestly rely upon and delegate strategic administrative tasks to the willing and talented individuals who assist them in achieving their business priorities. This vision will propel talented Assistants to greater heights around a common identity. I call this Exhilarating Vision Indispensability. To make this vision a reality, the Executive Assistant must acquire the skills and new knowledge necessary to respond to the shifting intelligence of the workplace.

The currency of the Executive Assistant is to master the science of achievement strategy. This requires consistent focus and consistent action. It is imperative that you focus on your goals instead of on the negative. You must connect with people, exercise step- by- step strategies and be unafraid to look at what is missing. Remember that we keep our power when we protect the power of others, when we make a difference in the life of another person. Together, these elements reinforce the creative qualities of this role and inspire excellence in all that you do. What you think, say, and do have to be the same. So, push beyond the envelope of your talent to the core of your character. Find your place to stand.

I invite you to take a moment to envision that you are the Executive. Now, imagine having "you" as his/her Assistant. I recommend that you practice this pleasant exercise when considering your role and purpose as a Strategic Support Specialist/Business Partner. There is no legacy in defending attitudes and skills of the past. The challenge is to courageously create your future and to appreciate that your skills and grace as Executive Life Managers impart calm influence.

In conversations with Executive Assistants, they express concern that without new knowledge to propel them to advance faster, they will become an untapped resource within their organizations. A key advancement strategy is to learn and apply frameworks that foster more effective decision-making.

We considered the premise that career development programs offer Executives a wide range of learning opportunities. It makes sense that those individuals who provide support to these Executives should be afforded the same opportunities to expand their capabilities. To remain relevant, it is important to go beyond mastering functional skills; Executive Assistants need an educational program that encapsulates the essential skills and knowledge necessary for analyses, decision-making, leadership, and management.

Executive Assistants who perform at the highest levels of their profession will have learned about international business and finance, and about international politics. The politically informed Assistant brings a new depth and breadth of understanding to the role. Assistants must acquire these skills to propel and maintain this career at the professional level and earn recognition as Strategic Support Specialists and Business Partners.

Remember that new learning is the best resource in the world. Remember that you do what you are. Remember that the life we live, and all of its events and relationships, are a reflection of ourselves. Hold fast Henry Ford's famous quote: "You can't build a reputation on what you are going to do."

We are never short of opportunity – opportunity appears and is created in every moment, at every moment.

As soon as you sit down to a cup of hot coffee, the Executive will ask you to do something which will last until the coffee is cold. A smile at someone you do not know, and may probably never see again, changes the face of the world. Our access to opportunity – and greatness – is always the result of right skills, right temperament, and right choices. Check your briefcase, make sure you have equal measures of all, and create and sustain your impact.

Sixty-Second Leadership©

Be Self-Aware: Externalize. Write down what you are thinking. Do not edit it or nice it up, just get it on the page. If you enjoy drawing, create a visual representation of your inner experience.

Be Self-Aware: Check your vital signs. Are you hungry, tired, stressed? Is it the end of a very long project? Is it just after lunch, and you are in a fog? We all get depleted. Be aware that your tank is low.

Be Self-Aware: Calibrate. Make it a point before every meeting to pause and calibrate your state on a scale of 0 to 5. 0 is "I am quite close to exploding." 5 is "I am poised, open hearted and curious." Don't judge, measure.

EQ/IQ CASE STORY – AN INTRODUCTION

In today's competitive job market, hiring managers are looking for one skill trait above all else: Emotional Intelligence (EI). The World Economic Forum's 2016 Future of Jobs report lists EI as a top 10 skill to possess among global new hires. A growing body of research, backed by leading behavioral scientists, points to EI as the single greatest nonmaterial asset of top performers in the workplace. This explains why hiring managers are narrowing their focus on how to identify a job candidate's level of EI. Part of being the emotionally intelligent Executive Assistant (EA) is having the nuanced ability to signal to others that we do, in fact, possess a high-level of EI. But how do we do this given the asset's nonmaterial value? Each Case Story explores a potential crisis and the application of Emotional Intelligence that drives its resolution.

In our case story, we will join Naveen, a professional Executive Assistant, throughout various points in her career. In our first story, Naveen has been selected to interview for a C-level Executive Assistant (EA) role at a FinTech startup. She knows that she needs to find a way to showcase her level of EI if she's going to succeed in impressing the hiring manager and meet and interview with the executive.

EQ/IQ Case Story 1: **The Emotionally Intelligent Candidate: Leading with Confidence.**

On her way to the interview, Naveen gathers her thoughts and readies her elevator pitch. She's been practicing this pitch, along with possible rounds of interview questions and answers. Whatever verbal and nonverbal criteria she had set and struggled to meet, such as speech patterns and body language, she has since made those adjustments and has perfected her delivery.

She arrives onsite no more than five minutes before her scheduled interview time and checks in with the front desk. The friendly Administrative Assistant offers one of several streamlined lobby chairs. Naveen chooses the chair closest to the front desk, just a few feet away from two, very tall, green-tinted glass doors. Steadying her nerves, she looks down at her crisp white shirt and jet-black suit, smoothing out the creases in her pants. A few minutes go by, which works to her benefit; she uses the time to put a finer point on the various interview scenarios that are about to take place. Five more minutes have passed.

Another ten minutes roll by – did she mistake the hiring manager's time request to interview? A ripple of dread resonates within her. Reaching for her bag, she pulls out her phone and verifies the e-mail correspondence between herself and the hiring manager. A slight cooling of relief; the time is correct. Looking up from her phone and to the front desk, she sees the assistant round the corner of her desk and make her way to Naveen. Bending down beside her, her voice slightly above a whisper, she relays the following, "Marta is running late. She extends her apologies. You'll be meeting with Scott instead. He'll be out as soon as his meeting wraps. Thank you for waiting." Naveen smiles and nods to the assistant. She thanks her, but deep inside Naveen can feel herself tighten. Scott is the Executive for whom she is being screened. She remembers the name when researching the company. Her nerves begin to fire; her body heats up; she can hear her breathing quicken, getting ever louder. Her preparation, her thoughts – her elevator pitch –

all have dissipated with the realization of having to meet an unexpected challenge. Her heartbeat, now pumping wildly, feels like its climbing up her throat, heading straight for her brain. Her anxiety is setting in, and she needs to get past it.

Her thoughts, like a digital flipbook, turn rapidly through myriad pages of stored information and then abruptly stop to reveal the pertinent information on emotional hijacking, the brain's danger response to negative stimulus, like job interview anxiety. When faced with this stimulus, emotional hijacking will force the brain to freeze its information center and prevent informed decision making from taking place. Because we feel before we think, Naveen's familiarity of this foundational understanding of EI has made her acutely aware of what she is feeling in response to being told that she is to meet with Scott: she is feeling fear, which is causing stress, because what lies beyond the glass doors is uncertain for her.

Self-identifying the emotion is step one to stopping emotional hijacking. Step two - accepting the emotion (in this case, the fear of uncertainty) is more thought-intensive but can be done with practice and habitual learning; both of which Naveen has committed herself to doing.

Her fear in response to the interview and the uncertainty of meeting Scott is unavoidable. She cannot hide from what is occurring in her head. And worrying as a means by which to analyze her fear and establish control is a short-term fix that will only serve to delay the fear. In fact, it can make it worse. If she is not worrying about being unprepared in meeting with Scott, she will start to worry about giving off the appearance of being unprepared.

Almost certainly, fear of bombing the interview will follow. Whatever coping fixes she employs for the first fear, a new one will emerge shortly thereafter, and it becomes a self-feeding worry loop.

This time, however, her knowledge of EI and awareness of the emotion that is causing the fear tells her what the long-term solution is to this unexpected challenge. Instead of worrying about her anxiety and trying to solve it, she decides to accept it.

The process of managing fear-induced anxiety is to identify it, accept it, and to move on from it. The key to beating emotional "hijacking" is to stop concentrating on the stimulus that is negative (i.e., the anxiety) and to start concentrating on the stimulus that is positive. Naveen can do this by concentrating on what she can control, her narrative, the professional story that she will share with Scott in her interview. She reminds herself that no matter who she meets with, Naveen is there to display who she is, and she is always prepared to do that. By shining a light on her authenticity, her *ideal* self will emerge.

This is how we tap into emotional confidence and endurance. When we use the emotions that are causing our emotional paralysis and turn them into emotional endurance, we not only reactivate the brain's information center, but also supercharge decision making; thereby, our ideal narratives can and will emerge. This is the third and final step of stopping emotional hijacking.

"Naveen?"

She blinks, her eyes focusing on the figure before her. This must be Scott. "Yes. Hello," she says back to him.

"Sorry to keep you waiting," he says with a smile, "It's been one of those days. Come on back." He turns from her, walks over to open one of the green-tinted glass doors, keeping it open for her to walk through.

The Takeaway. We are physiologically prewired to *feel* first. The interplay that exists between the brain's emotional center, the amygdala, and its information center, the prefrontal cortex, has us feeling emotion before thinking and responding to it. Not surprisingly, having an acute sense of emotional awareness and management is important for several reasons. Executive Assistants who have mastered their emotions are more likely to stay calm under pressure, adapt to adverse conditions, form higher-functioning partnerships, communicate with empathy, maintain positive outlooks, and solve complex problems.

The Toolkit. When we feel our emotions starting to get the best of us, remember, we can apply the following toolkit to train ourselves into having more control over our states of mind in times of uncertainty.

- Recognize the cause: Understanding the origins of our emotional responses and accepting those responses reduces their perceived harm. You see, the brain cannot tell the difference between triggers that are physically menacing and those that are mentally intimidating, but the emotionally intelligent, self-aware Executive Assistant can. Accepting nervousness for what it is, the brain's natural alarm system with emotional histories tied to our ancestors' early survival, takes away its power and returns it back to you, where it belongs.

- Reframe your mindset.
  - Notice the behavior you wish to change. Mild, anxious feelings are temporary signals that something within us requires our attention and careful thought. Having this awareness enables the reframing process, one training session at a time.
  - Acknowledge your real self. The emotionally intelligent mind is a trustworthy source of information, not our primitive brains.
  - Articulate your goal.
  - Choose your ideal self.
- Retain your story: Manage short-term anxiety in a healthy way by proving it wrong and facing it head on. A small amount of nervous feelings can be turned into something positive, like improving the job interview experience. The next time we feel pressured to perform, let's concentrate that anxious energy into communication that is warm, friendly, and moderately assertive. Spreading these positive emotions has a resounding effect, adding a deeper layer of meaning to the conversation than words alone. Instead of nervousness, we're mood sharing transmissible feelings of optimism and confidence, informing both the speaker (you) and the listener (in this case, the interviewer) how we should be feeling in that moment.

The Application. Identify the emotion. Accept the emotion. Guide the response. Consciously putting into practice these efforts can transmute the emotional stimulus that is causing the hijacking/paralysis and turn it into emotional endurance, a hallmark characteristic of the best Executive Assistants, worldwide.

CHAPTER IV

What Is the Executive Assistant Success Model?

If you love the work of Executive Assisting, the only way to approach this career is with joy and camaraderie. If it is your core passion, then you know *how* to get things done with Executive-like confidence because you know *why* you do *what* you do. Self-awareness, self-knowledge, and self-management are key.

Assistants: You know *why* you are important to your company's success. Take personal accountability for acquiring the capabilities required to strengthen your Business Partner relationship status. You cannot be a Strategic Business Partner if you can't cope. Make sure you know what you have signed up for, and why.

Yes, you are totally committed to improving efficiency through continuous improvement, good problem-solving brain power, and a commitment to quality. You understand your responsibilities and how meeting them impacts your Executives and your company's performance. You possess the experience of knowing how to do things well, knowing which things should be done in the first place, and which should not.

Here is the challenge: *more is required*. The expectation is that you must be able to connect across businesses, divisions and regions in ways that create new techniques to promote high-quality decisions and lightning-fast execution.

Your present skillset accomplishes all of this, so how is it that more is required? Because there is the undeniable (and unavoidable) impact of economic disruptions, with non-stop change, and major demographic shifts caused by generational differences. These changes have real implications for how employers and employees work together. Simultaneously, workplace changes connected to technology continue to intensify.

Studies reveal that CEOs are responding by giving operational innovation a prominent place on their agendas and identifying "critical talent" within the ranks of their organizations. This is the content and context of your role; you embody the content of innovation daily, and one of the most important pieces of context in this role is that you get tested along the way. It's no surprise that you are placed in this "critical talent" category.

Mobility in your role has expanded. So, what are the skills that are translatable to success?

Your strength is in your ability and desire to solve complex problems every moment of every day. This is rewarding work that requires focus and intention; and it is a dramatic departure from the commonly defined Executive Assistant role, that has historically denied accomplished and rightly-motivated Professional Assistants the opportunity to exercise their potential. Assistants today have the determination and commitment to excel and to invest in improving at everything they do. This remains their (*your*) top priority.

Your strategic approach is your winning suit; you are a Specialist and a Generalist. Your objective shifts and changes with every innovation in technology or in business strategy. Often, you are working with a given direction and a blank page from which to create the intent, design the structure, build the team and accept responsibility for the outcome. You know the difference between efficiency (doing things right) and effectiveness (doing the right things). You know the difference between important and immediate.

Your responsibility, therefore, begins with a commitment to quality. Make sure that you have the tools you need to be effective; that the value of your work is acknowledged and is tied to the goals of the Executive(s) you support and to the strategy of your company; and that you remain fully engaged.

Managing Executive expectations is the art and science of the work of the Assistant. It is the key to Executive Assistant productivity through high-performance standards, techniques and strategies that facilitate a healthy perspective in the Executive/Executive Assistant Business Partnership. Most Senior Executives now rely more than ever on their Administrative Quarterback, who fills the roles of their "advance person," and their "right-hand-person." They almost always have a single individual on staff whose job it is to serve as troubleshooter, translator, help desk attendant, diplomat, human database, weather advisor, travel consultant, sales executive, amateur psychologist, spousal interface, and ambassador to the inside and outside world (as the need arises).

Who better than you? You have absolute drive, a competitive edge that elevates you, and you stay focused on what is important. You invest in yourself for the benefit of others. With knowledge and experience, you are both expert and ally. You project a positive image, plan everything with attention and care, and you do what you enjoy. You exercise prudent political judgment, which is a good measure of your credibility. And above all, you are empathetic.

With active, living intelligence – Emotional Intelligence – and the values of self-knowledge and self-management, you effortlessly sail through these dynamic challenges:

Providing tactical and strategic support...

> ...allows you to streamline processes with detailed precision and create structure.

Being empathetic...

> ...calls you to diffuse the anxiety of the person you support. You are able to find the right words for difficult situations and provide emotional support.

Managing...

> ...helps you to sustain an effective work-environment during times of chaos and create order out of complex processes.

Performing with certitude...

>...offers you the opportunity to sprint through this ever-changing business environment.

Learning and applying knowledge...

>...illustrates that you appreciate the culture of your organization, your role in it, and your Executive's role in it, and that you know how things get done.

Inspiring trust...

>...the product of effectively self-managing allows Executives to focus more strategically.

And you can rest assured that the impact of your emotional intelligence is strengthened by the depth and breadth of your existing skills. These following skills do more than showcase the quality of your work – they showcase the quality of your character:

Common Sense: Remember that common sense is not so common, but always needed; bring it to every interaction.

Communication skills: We all know good communication is not just what you say, but how you say it. If you are responsive, gracious, and humble, if you speak decisively and are gifted in making a point, your authenticity will always shine through.

Interpersonal skills: Your authenticity allows your "response-ability" to be fully expressed. Embrace being the person who people call when they are "not sure who to call"; the person who is ready with an answer, and doubly ready to find one if needed. Seize every opportunity to add human content to business context.

Critical-thinking skills: Your ability to anticipate "next steps" and to apply small, well-thought-out ideas to the bigger picture confirm that you are more than just practical – you are approachable.

Organizational and time allocation skills: You have a system for keeping track of multiple projects, tasks and deadlines (and it works!). You are able to set priorities and work effectively. Don't underestimate the sense of security you instill simply by demonstrating how any mountain can be climbed one step at a time.

Leadership skills: You can spot talent, communicate expectations, and inspire performance. You are tactful. You believe in your own leadership ability – as will your colleagues; your business-practical skillset helps create an atmosphere of trust in both what you do and who you are.

Remember Mark Twain's famous quote: "The two most important days in your life are the day you are born and the day you find out why." Here's an example.

In a cover letter that accompanied a resume, a candidate wrote the following: "I am a graceful but firm gatekeeper, a concise orator, and a loyal and intuitive confidant. I have developed a will to manage, an ability to proactively pull together a day before it unfolds, and an intuitive sense of how to react to changing corporate landscapes; quickly mastering any new learning curve and making it look effortless."

"I know where my executives are at all times; I understand their goals and who is important to them, and who needs to be held at a distance. My to-do lists are eternal and that is a comfort to me. Having grown up in an area with few resources, I am accustomed to being prepared, practicing patience and reacting with intelligence to changes in the landscape.

"I am passionate about what I do," the author continues, "and I know that an Executive Assistant will always be far more than just a person who performs a Puritanical execution of chores. They will be called on for their insight and intelligence in navigating matters, making observations and solving problems; and for their personal effectiveness, which is the capacity to follow through and get the right things done."

Executives: Executive Assistants participate and thrive in the same business arena as you, expertly navigating highly networked markets, global organizations, and the expanding presence of information technology. Change is the only constant in an Assistant's day, which is full to the brim with incoming information, split-second decision-making, efficiency assessments and prioritization, and making time where there is none. Recognizing the extraordinary degree of skill, intelligence, adaptability and grace it takes to achieve success under these circumstances is an integral element in appropriately measuring your Assistant's contributions.

Assistants: It is not surprising that you have realized such rich continuity in a global business universe that challenges Executives to accomplish more with fewer resources. In this rapid-cycle economy that demands the capacity and willingness to change, organizational leaders are relying on skilled professionals, like you, and positioning them as indispensable members of senior leadership teams around the world.

Remember: Create your own future! We might say that in order for us to compete, in order to make the short term meet the long term, what remains is for us to pursue a personal strategy concept that focuses on updating and learning new skills. Personal growth can be achieved through vocational development to acquire new skills. The road ahead requires professional courage, strategic competence and intellectual integration.

So, what is the one thing you can alter this week to expand your career? Remember, do not be afraid to look at what is missing. The gaps in skills are easy to detect and hard to ignore.

I find it curious that companies continue to search for top level Executive Assistants who bring the global business knowledge required for superb performance; yet, do not provide the time-opportunity or financial support to offer the required level of education. or the appropriate compensation, to these key individuals. The question that comes to mind is: Why not? The answer is found in informed self-management.

Sixty-Second Leadership©

A Test in Confidence: "Too Much to Do"

The People. Lauren has been an Executive Assistant at her company for two years. Her primary responsibility is to support Patrick, an underwriting officer. She also provides assistance to other staff. Patrick's career at the company spans 25 years. Lauren is still learning Patrick's personality and management style. Patrick has a clear vision of the direction that he would like to take the division. He can't do it without help.

The Situation. Next week's meetings in the US Virgin Islands were rescheduled by the client a few weeks ago. Patrick suddenly realizes that the flight itineraries haven't been revised accordingly. He wants to say something to Lauren about this but holds back. He thinks: "I hate to ask Lauren to do things. She's so reserved – she's quiet, almost cold sometimes. I sometimes feel as if I'm micromanaging when I remind her of something that is a priority. It's easier to just get things done myself."

Lauren did see the notice about the change in the meeting date but wanted to ask Patrick about his flight preferences. Patrick was out of the office at the time.

On this particular day, Lauren tells Patrick that she's exhausted. She's been completely absorbed in managing details for the upcoming Executive retreat to be held in Connecticut. She tells Patrick that she needs a short break, maybe a half hour to get some air. Patrick, in the midst of writing e-mails behind stacks of reports and letters to be sent, nods his head, hiding his irritation. He thinks, "When I began my career, I wouldn't have taken a break during the busiest part of the day – or I would have first asked my supervisor if anything urgent needed to be done."

Another Administrative Professional stops by. She asks where Lauren is. Patrick wants to call Lauren on her cell but hesitates to interrupt her break. Patrick asks, "Is it important?" The reply, "It's okay, I'll send her a text message. She responds quickly."

Patrick thinks: "I should be glad that Lauren makes herself useful to other staff. She works hard (even though I'm never exactly sure on what). She's smart, a nice kid. But she doesn't seem invested. If she cared, I'd take her on the next few trips so she could learn what we do, first-hand."

Outside, Lauren runs into Amir, an Assistant from another department. She chats with him: "I've been on this job for only two years. I am amazed at how much I have to do on my own. Patrick's always traveling – but when he's in, all of a sudden, I have to drop everything to deal with his stuff. This really messes me up. He just doesn't get it, how I keep the office running. I'm the only one who knows the procedures for just about everything in the division. I'm the one who shows the ropes to new people; managing interns, training temps, and making sure there's coverage at all times."

Lauren sighs. "I wish Patrick appreciated me more. He's barely around, and always in a hurry. I'm afraid to say anything to him, there's so much to do before he leaves. Like tonight – I have to stay late to get paperwork filed so that the contractor can repair the cabinetry in his office next week. And who knows what Patrick will expect me to do before he leaves for his next trip. It's as if I'm supposed to read his mind."

Lauren glances at her watch. "Uh-oh, I have to leave!"

She waves goodbye to Amir and returns to the office – just as Patrick finishes making his new flight reservations, leaving the receptionist with instructions to double-check the hotel bookings.

Questions:

- What does Lauren communicate to Patrick in her self-presentation?
- What does Lauren *not* communicate?
- What might be obstacles to better communication between Lauren and Patrick?
- Are Lauren and Patrick in conflict? Do they have common interests?
- How can Lauren exercise creative problem solving and leadership to make this a win-win situation – and to have a better job experience?

EQ / IQ

CHAPTER V

Unmasking the Archetype

Some of you may remember Jane Hathaway, the loyal and efficient secretarial assistant to the banker, Milburn Drysdale, in the long-running TV program, the *Beverly Hillbillies*. She became one of the modern-day American archetypes from which our current idea of the role of assistant is fashioned.

While Ms. Hathaway was flawlessly prim, meticulously coiffed, impeccably presented and always ready to serve, we find that today's Executive Assistant is projected as more relaxed, calm, still, effective and, in keeping with the age of social media, more externally engaged.

Comparing Jane Hathaway to our present-day professional Executive Assistant allows us to recalibrate and identify the clearest and most accurate ideas about the intellectual legitimacy of this role. We challenge the out-of-date ideas, and bring to light the masses of experience, while we translate this position description to the prominence it implies. Archetypes and by extension, stereotypes, present opportunities! Why? They urge us to examine divergent views from actual reality.

There is a distinction that embodies the emergent role of the Executive Assistant. That distinction is the difference between supporting the Executive and holding the space of the Executive you support as an integral Business Partner. My thirty-five years of experience tells me that neither the archetypical Miss Hathaway, nor the modern-day Assistant (as currently projected), embrace the true scope, range and nuance of this critical position. Neither projection – dare I say "stereotype" – allows for, nor acknowledges, the type of integral and integrated Executive/Executive Assistant Business Partnership. This is a relationship that is fueled by a demand for success in an ever-changing, competitive global economy.

The Executive Assistant population differs in personality, temperament, experience, intellect, age, education, upbringing, values, and beliefs. Collectively, you have earned a stellar reputation; individually, you are highly interesting people, who by extensive experience know that intellectual leadership, strategic support skills and organizational influence have promoted upward mobility and created superb results.

I have a rising optimism for Executive Assistant support teams when I consider the relevance and strategic importance of this role. The new emphasis on appropriate job titles suggests that this is a time of heightened responsibility and greater career accountability.

We are entering an exciting new period in human history, where creativity, ingenuity and global thinking are the three top leadership skills ranked by CEOs. For Executive Assistants, the current time presents unparalleled professional challenge; yet it also offers remarkable opportunities. Focusing productively on professional adaptability, personal development, and your own career growth will help you to adapt to what's ahead. There is much to be enthusiastic about. Let's look at a few emerging trends and resultant needs.

There are two visions: the first vision is that the emerging role of the Executive Assistant requires precise execution, with equal parts of trust and timing, and a range of attributes, perspective, empathy, and prior knowledge. I see everything from the perspective of defining this role as a profession. This will take courage, a willingness to change points of view, and intellectual power.

The Executive Assistant – the Executive Liaison – the Executive Life Manager – is now trusted with even more responsibility: technology, if anything, has made you more essential than ever. Technology has allowed users faster execution; but technology does not manage personal interface, nor does it prioritize business needs. Even the most advanced business intelligence applications can't pose challenging questions. Often the most compelling data for business decisions comes through a high-level interpersonal dynamic. Executive Assistants enable strong leaders to stay focused because they can see a problem, brief the Executive and offer possible solutions. Companies who value the Executive-Executive Assistant Business Partnership relationships achieve scalable benefits.

Truly, there will never be an adequate substitute for an aware, invested, and diligent human being, one who knows and can sensibly weigh the gravity of every aspect of a company. Effective persons in top management acknowledge this in their reliance on a competent Executive Assistant. What is perhaps less acknowledged is the rapid rate in which the scope of responsibility grows – unlike computers, Executive Assistants today must have an infinitely expanding "hard drive" in order to provide necessary support. The difficulty in defining this role reflects the strategic skillset required to efficiently and effectively manage the function of Executive Life Manager. Salaries and bonuses at these levels must range within Executive-level baselines, and those in support positions with C-Suite trajectories should also be in line to receive the appropriate amount of compensation.

Assisting management, in today's climate, *is* managing. Consider just how much of an Executive Assistant's role hinges on solidifying elements that can only be described as "fluid" – time, location, technology; these ever-changing components must somehow be wrestled into the frame of schedules, itineraries, and contingency plans. Not "if possible;" they *must*.

In this tactical role, you are gauged by success, not by intention. How seriously should we take this idea? Quite seriously! A solid resume and a great work ethic are not enough.

Executives are facing unmet needs as they struggle to find individuals in the Executive support role, with the ability to bring global and business knowledge and advanced technology applications to this position. This requires new skills and advanced business knowledge that will outperform the traditional Executive Support role.

Now, Executive Assistants are expected to focus on results, think like managers, maximize efficiency, have excellent analytic skills, and the tenacity to reduce complexity to simplicity. Assistants will have to both get it right and think the right way. The quality of decisions and the ability to deliver successful outcomes are what make the Assistant valuable; new learning is essential. Now, we are in new territory, which assures Executive Assistant advantage: With the goalposts always moving, and most of us not knowing what to expect next, why does the Executive Assistant continue to emerge as one of the most important hires in any company, in any industry, anywhere in the world? I offer that it is because you are informed by your experience that preparation is 99% of taking advantage of the right opportunity.

There have been radical changes in the implied contract between employer and employee. The days when only a few people at the top had to concern themselves with issues of profitability are over. The organizations that thrive will do so by developing generalists who are well-suited to the task of keeping up with new developments and helping the organization to quickly deliver value. The individuals who thrive will be those who incorporate a certain entrepreneurial outlook, no matter what the nature of their work or their formal job title.

In addition to such alterations of first principles, there have been important changes in the structure of the successful organization. Previously, information was concentrated in the hands of the few, and pyramid-like hierarchical structures promoted efficient operations from the top down. In today's business environment, information is so widely dispersed, and competition is so fierce, that everyone in the organization must contribute "field intelligence," and new ideas, that will further the aim of satisfying a diverse customer base.

The second vision is that while business leaders search for categories of growth, Executive Assistants look for new areas of possibility. Reassess how you can add value. Strengthen your persuasive and influence-based skills. To achieve a skills goal, ask yourselves: How can I develop capabilities that meet and exceed expectations? In what ways can I simplify processes and develop the agility required to execute rapidly?

The Executive Assistant is often the person who must determine what updates from the front and proposed new initiatives are worth immediate review by top Executives. Knowing the difference between what is important and what is immediate carries immense implications for an organization's ability to carry out its mission.

The Executive Assistant, then, has become one of the most critical people on the entire flow chart – an important power center in the organization. You are both on the first line of technological implementation and information management, and you are also privy to the most important strategic initiatives in the organization. Such a role is not for those who prefer narrow job descriptions and clear-cut answers to all questions. Today, the role of Executive Assistant requires a person with foresight, great adaptability, a particular kind of commitment and a specialized strength required to occupy the position.

In this key role, communication, always a vital skill, takes on more importance than ever. Those who thrive in the coming years will commit to ongoing personal and professional development in this area. You are compelled by your areas of responsibility to develop and refine your effectiveness as a communicator with others in the organization.

Of supreme importance is the willingness and ability to develop competence in dealing with a business world marked by ambiguity, uncertainty, and constant reinvention. A sense of balance amidst turmoil is essential. The "big picture" is subject to constant revision, and, often, the Executive Assistant is the first to realize that a course correction is necessary.

Change, however, need not mean chaos. It can mean opportunity. The challenge we face lies in finding the most effective way to facilitate the changes that must occur, to draw up appropriate plans of action that will put our organizations – and, not coincidentally, our own careers – at an advantage. Unparalleled opportunity awaits those who embrace change.

Rapid technological change and global integration of the U.S. economy directly impacts today's workforce. What it means to be an "effective Executive" has become both more broad and more nuanced than ever before. Predictably, so has the role of supporting the Executive been affected. We know that Executive Assistants certainly have more to manage, and we cannot ignore the opportunities this presents. Each new challenge is an occasion to showcase your adaptability, knowledge, experience, and value; a chance to expand and advance in your role. Today's business climate can only be mastered by proactively meeting changing trends and by applying our previously discussed Four Pillars: Intuition, Initiative, Innovation, Integrity, to which we add Insight.

These trends (globalization, technological innovation, demographic shifts, economic uncertainty, and process innovation) have important implications that are particularly relevant in today's business environment. They are the key indicators of performance tracking. We are experiencing a dramatic workplace transformation, with a particular emphasis on demographic shifts.

Employees with dissimilar values, approaches and philosophies about work have always existed. For the first time in history, five diverse generations are working side-by-side, and often colliding. Generational differences can affect everything, including rewards, communication and ultimately productivity. This phenomenon is reshaping the business agenda in the public and private sectors everywhere.

Overcoming age discrimination is one persevering stereotype. Some have argued that older individuals are more likely to be burned out; that they are resistant to new technologies; that there are frequent absences due to illness, that they are not effective at working with younger supervisors; that they are reluctant to travel; they are less creative, less productive, slower mentally, more expensive to employ.

Here's the wildly divergent view: Some suggest that older employees soundly outperform their younger colleagues; that every aspect of job performance gets better as we age. It is reported that older workers score high in leadership, detail-oriented tasks, organization, listening, writing and problem-solving skills. Apparently, less-tenured staff needs to commit to meet the standards set by experienced staff and experienced staff needs to be collaborative and inspire strong communication.

Managing differences through collaboration is the central challenge of a globalized workplace business strategy. Diversity has progressed from being a perceived handicap to becoming a recognized competitive advantage. A critical measure of Executive Assistant excellence intersects at interpersonal management and the ability to create symmetry out of chaos. Workplace diversity in all its stereotypical representations is offset by the skill of Empathy. We again emphasize that this is the foundation for a collaborative workplace and is among the subtle distinctions that define the extraordinary Executive Assistant. It is an aspect of your organizational influence.

"Empathy is a skill that allows us to be tolerant and capable of dealing effectively with a wide variety of people", says Daniel Goleman in his popular book, *Emotional Intelligence*. Empathy, then, is a necessary – dare I say *critical* – communication skill as we wrestle with the realities and challenges of global integration. Nothing reaches across the entire domain of Executive Assistant support as does this vital skill. It is hard to make a credible claim of effective Executive management if you do not have the capability to demonstrate the ability to understand and support others with compassion or sensitivity. Empathy changes your thinking and your language.

Empathy is the sustaining skill for success. It doesn't mean you have to agree with how others see things; rather being empathetic means you are willing and able to appreciate what the other person is experiencing. Empathy requires listening, nonjudgmental openness and emotional intelligence. It is an important factor in relationships; it is positively related to job performance. Empathy is a life skill. It is a social goal.

Your Predictive Power

As previously stated, the Boss/Subordinate structure has become an archaic system. Rather, Executive Assistants are strong business allies, with a real share in the purpose and mission of the organization. What does this mean? It means everyone needs a co-pilot.

The world is changing, and tough economic times require "focus," execution and the ability to innovate. The search for new ideas is the new business model. Your strategic advantage is that while you are responding to these operational changes, the content and context of your role will be more diverse, challenging and rewarding than ever before.

That isn't to say that reaping the benefits of change will be effortless. Those who do this work must have the endurance capacity to sustain themselves in environments where they will encounter: uneven temperaments and pace-disrupting behavior, a greater urgency for speed and accuracy, limited signs of appreciation, conflicting instructions, and (as always) a demand for high levels of intelligence and superb response skills. Executive Assistants must have the ability to manage distracted behaviors, both their own and from others; you cannot operate effectively in a world of excuses. So, make sure you know what you are signing up for, and why. Understand that it comes at a price; a price which has its rewards.

The current administrative support model focuses on all the talents you would expect of the Executive Assistant – opportunities abound, and well beyond traditional Executive care. Now, there is a blurring of the lines between strategic administrative support and role-related management responsibilities. Remember our "Architecture of Support": *Leadership*, *Management*, and *Strategic Support*. These three dimensions define the evolving Executive Assistant profile and characterize the Executive/Executive Assistant Business Partnership. The central thesis is that these business skills are distinct from traditional skills. The distinction is valid.

Efficient Executive Assistants provide support to Executives by being able to truly see and hear what is going on at the surface, as well as under the surface. *Effective* Executive Assistants are guided by knowing what is important to the Executive, then managing accordingly. *Influential* Assistants support the Executive on critical, interpersonal matters by applying a special set of skills to influence people's emotions, feelings, and attitudes.

Taking on a Leader's role demands the ability to help Executives to achieve their goals. Leaders on the front line must anticipate what is new and changing, requiring focus several years into the future. Assuming the Manager's role means that you are the reminder, and the strategic supporter, to balance today's pressure and longer-term accomplishments.

Efficient Strategic Support: I cannot emphasize enough that process improvements require new learning to understand that when a system changes, you must change the way you think about it. Executive Assistants need these new tools.

Today's business leaders continue to be faced with workforce issues, regulatory concerns and globalization. And the choices they make affect the workplaces we all inhabit. The old way of managing the Executive Assisting role must be transformed by learning how things can be done better and faster. The road ahead requires professional courage, strategic competence and intellectual integration. This is the serious business of the Executive Assistant.

You fill several different roles, from writer to stage manager to director. It can be a vast and complex responsibility, one that requires an offensive and a defensive posture. You are not tyrannized by distractions or by the urgent. You can rebound and play great defense so that everyone rallies.

Pursuing the role of Executive Assisting is to engage in a study in human behavior. It is neither a race to obtain the higher ground, nor is it an exercise in being guarded or entitled. The playing field must be even at all times, with both parties (Executive and Assistant) willingly open with, and aware of, the conditions and collaborations necessary for success.

The general principle we find is that this is an Executive-level career that requires intellectual compatibility with the

Executive you support. Everything you thought you knew about assisting is changing in order to respond to ongoing events that are revolutionizing the very nature of work. The best thing is to keep learning. A focus on leadership principles adds value. Let's consider these as required tools: Vision. Innovation. Creativity. Also imperative is a sense of humor to diffuse tensions in tough situations, along with the character qualities of honesty and ethics.

One way to manage your progress is to chart a development course, which includes three overlapping principles: Personal Style, Professional Judgment, and Self-Management:

Personal Style: You have the personal responsibility for refining your skill sets, improving your knowledge base, enriching your relationship with Executives, and promoting your relationship with your colleagues.

Professional Judgment: The digitized office now has transformed the traditional desk into an Executive command center at which the Executive Assistant sits in control

Self-Management: Your ability to self-manage is the source of your personal power. It forces you to squarely confront your own limitations and motives, and to accept the challenge of working to improve your own qualities.

If you are managing yourself effectively, you will remain open to the possibility of doing things differently, and you will learn to laugh at yourself and the outrageous circumstances you encounter. Pick one limitation that you know about yourself and consciously act to alter your propensities – and see what happens.

In this new economic order, particular attention must be given to acquiring, applying and sustaining your indispensable workplace skills. Anything you do at work is an improve-able skill, from the most basic to the most challenging. It is in our work, above all, that the most obvious and most tangible opportunities for personal development exist.

What is the cost to participating in new learning? A commitment to time. Let me remind you of the four viewpoints for creating and delivering value: the FIRST is that a new performance responsibility has emerged; the SECOND point is that the willingness to change is a key strength; thus, thinking becomes the new commodity; the THIRD is that your role is important as you focus on results and maximize efficiency; and the FOURTH is that as you accept higher levels of responsibility within your role, your work will be most critical to creating a high-performance environment. It is about volume and pace.

What is the benefit? You will be viewed throughout the organization as someone with broad business knowledge and a great a sense of how the Executive wants things done. You will be an effective Manager.

You will now have a greater oversight role; you will be expected to manage the process, control the flow of people and paper, while adjusting to different business styles. You will have to manage the flow of information to and from the Executive, understanding, categorizing and relating expectations even under difficult and tight deadlines, from crisis to crisis. You will outline priorities, strategies and plans for execution. This is a position where the end, and how you get there, matters. You must now innovate, not replicate. You must embrace challenges, while offering worthy alternatives.

Your position is indispensable, invaluable, important, and always will be essential. Don't be imprisoned by your job description. Self-awareness, self-management, social awareness (empathy), relationship management and enthusiasm promote successful job performance in today's high-power cultures.

What is the pay out to the Assistant (beyond sainthood and going to Heaven in the afterlife)? Finding satisfaction in the work that you do, and performing in your high-performance zone, is your ultimate payout! Hope and expectation are not a "plan"! Executive Assisting is a learning profession. We must move the ball of new learning up the field. Accept the global mandate and enhance your credibility by welcoming opportunities for continuing education, ongoing training and the acquisition and implementation of new skills. This is your work challenge.

Remember that you – and you alone – are responsible for developing your career. To get ahead and build a satisfying future, you must become your own brand and be your own CEO. Remember that a personal strategy is comparable to a business strategy: you must have a clear mission. Plan and assess your results. Remember that you have to change to adapt; recognize the impact of technology; own your core competencies; enjoy a reputation for ethical standards and integrity and focus on the long term.

Remember that old ideas are our biggest liability – we can either blindly (or stubbornly) adhere to them, or seek out new and better ways to approach each challenge. Which would you prefer in the middle of the ocean: an anchor, or a boat? Remember that the path to *your* success is paved by *your* decisions. Remember that the amount of education you have determines your economic destiny. Remember that we cannot attain our highest potential selves without discipline and training.

Here's the takeaway – in shorthand: that a new perspective, a new optimism, and a new respect for the Executive Assistant position is taking hold! Some stereotypes (Jane Hathaway) only capture a moment in time – *at that moment in time* – and quickly fade to nostalgia. The role of the professional Executive Assistant always evolves and always will be indispensable. This career is here to stay.

CHAPTER VI

Executives: Here's Why You Need to Pay Attention to This! Who Is the Executive Assistant?

A strategic colleague. The person who you call in the middle of the night when you have an idea or a task that you want executed first thing in the morning. The person who greets you the next morning (having arrived at the crack of dawn) reassuring you that the task has been handled; that the most effective course of action (that works with your calendar and relieves you of multiple conversations on the same topic) was to arrange a video-conference so that you can communicate your idea to your global marketing team. This is the person who enables you to meet the challenges of the global business landscape. This is the person whose strategic decisions save you and others' time. This person's unquestionable value is in the ability to perform as your daily, minute-by-minute problem-solver.

The Purpose of the Role: A Profound Sense of Mission.

The purpose of the Executive Assistant is to offer techniques and ideas that add the most value and demonstrate a commitment to delivering at the highest levels of performance. Executive Assistants are not tyrannized by the urgent. They manage for strategic effectiveness.

Executive success is dependent upon talented Executive Assistants. They represent a strong business function whose purpose is to focus on accomplishing the goals that meet the needs of the Executive and the company. They are among any company's critical talent population. Why? They provide administrative stability, the discipline to do more things better, and the skills to manage the magnitude of systems with consistency, reliability, and focus.

Executive Assistants' strategic skill is to provide the basis for Executives to make the best-informed decisions possible. They conduct due diligence in order to assure that all relevant information is available to aid in the decision process, and with exactly the right level of detail. Thorough and balanced preparation of such materials is the responsibility of experienced Executive Assistants.

The Professional Executive Assistant is entrusted to make the Executive's vision a reality. The most valued Executive Assistant is the person who aligns his/her strategy with the Executive's and the organization's mission. Those who do this work well know that the key is in the orientation of the role. There must be personal chemistry between the Executive and the Assistant. Executive Assistants' intellectual and technical capabilities are influences; yet, it is the "personality fit factor" that is the key to sustainable performance, both personally and organizationally. Each must like, respect and trust the other, and have the friendship-based capacity to apply humor to challenging situations. Mutual respect, accountability, trust, and adaptability must be absolute.

Why Do You Need an Executive Assistant?

When you stop and think about it, Executives will realize that the work performed by Executive Assistants is probably some of the most varied and intellectually challenging work in the entire company. And much of what they do parallels what a good Executive does: they shape the broad picture into a set of action steps, and then they execute!

The demand on the time and energy of Senior Executives has been escalating rapidly in a period of globalization, economic disruption, financial distress, and increasing competition from every source. Executives who know the value of, and can leverage, a great Executive Assistant can propel their company and their careers. Executive Assistants are the professionals who by extensive experience know the difference between not letting things go unnoticed and not letting things go unchecked. This specifies the conditions for their success. The importance of this distinction cannot be overstated.

Conscious Executives acknowledge the immeasurable value offered by a devoted ally who operates on the same wavelength. This is the person who can take anxiety out of the Executive's day, and support and manage the Executive's business goals. Someone whose intimate knowledge of the Executive's day-to-day (both business and personal) compels their efforts to alleviate the overwhelming burden these responsibilities present. Someone who, with tact, intelligence, and diplomacy, is a tenacious inquisitor – one whose personal investment in the company informs both their ability to gather critical information for the company's success and their knowledge of how to use it. Someone who is not merely a shadow or reflection, but a companion walking the same road, willing and able to overcome the same obstacles.

There are three critical dimensions to hiring and working more effectively with Executive Assistants. First is the Executive's willingness to invest the time and effort to consider what aspects of his/her workload can be assumed or restructured into segments that can be managed by his or her Assistant. Second, the Executive Assistant's willingness to stretch beyond his/her comfort zone in order to assume new and more complex responsibilities and consistently produce results. Third, the Executive Assistant's ability as manager to remain persistent, tough-minded, hardworking, intelligent, and analytical.

What should you look for when hiring a Professional Executive Assistant?

I. Performance Skills:

o Experience (*How has the person expanded in the role?*)

o Competencies (*What are the areas in which this person excels?*)

o Personal Attributes (*Does this person reflect confidence and a centered ego; someone who gets it done?*)

- Knowledge (*Does this person have the reliable skills?*)
- Social/Interpersonal Skills (*Does this person have the charisma to manage global relationships?*)

II. CSI:

- Character: Professional Courage (*the intention to do the right thing*)
- Strategic Competence (*knowing how to do the right thing*)
- Imagination: Intellectual Integration (*the ability to deliver and execute the right thing*)

What exactly does the Professional Executive Assistant do?

The expert Professional Executive Assistant focuses on results and on maximizing efficiency. The Assistant understands the importance of clarifying the employer's objectives by putting himself/herself in those situations and applying good judgment. The goal is to weed through ambiguity, manage inherent unpredictability, zero in on the most important points, reach a decision and execute on behalf of the Executive. The key is to have the ability to connect unrelated questions or ideas to an unexpected event.

The Secret of a Great Executive Assistant

The secret of a great Executive Assistant is the principle of attitude, the breadth of collaboration, and attention to detail. This is an experienced individual whose judgment, creativity and skill saves Executives' time (which impacts company revenue and expenses) and expands Executive span of control (which directly impacts Executive efficiency). Most Executive Assistants are strategically positioned, but the most effective are also empowered to act strategically.

The gateway to accomplishment for strategic Executive Assistants is to be able to find errors, theirs and others, and to correct them; to manage a calendar and complex travel with judgment and common sense; to juggle personal and professional relationships; and to apply the dictates of probability. Professional life for Executive Assistants is a matter of probabilities; the predictable is seldom the outcome. The ability to deal with ambiguity, uncertainty and change is the value added to Executive productivity and success. So, professional Executive Assistants plan accordingly, read and digest all information that crosses theirs and Executives' desks, then highlight and bring to Executives' attention the essential points, all the while integrating this information into their own thinking: how to prioritize each day's events; knowing relationships inside and outside the organization and managing all such relationships with poise and confidence; acquiring a keen sense of where problems are most likely to be and with whom, and then integrating that confidential information into all planning and executing of tasks.

Executive Assistants display incredible intellectual agility and situational flexibility in their daily work: Their capacity to field and manage rapid-fire demands is a testament to their broad talents and skillset; their accuracy and finesse when decision-making underscores their informed wisdom; and their application of mind and method across a range of changing circumstances borders on athletic.

Additionally, smart Assistants pay attention to clues in the Executive's behavior and shifts in temperament, because timing and judgment are the foundation of a smooth working relationship. This helps Assistants not to take information passed on at face value, or to make assumptions in their decision making. Why? Because they know that priorities and concerns change, and that they have to be on top of these shifts all the time.

Defining the Business Partnership

Often the Executive Assistant most resembles Executives themselves by mastering the art of delegation and exercising fluid, decisive action. While the Executive Assistant's role will continue to be defined in relation to the Executive's responsibilities and the structure and culture of the organization, in this new world economy, the work of the Executive Assistant is placed squarely in the middle of the work of the Executive. This is an opportunity for the Executive/Executive Assistant Business Partnership to exceed past accomplishments and enter new territory by incorporating different renditions of the role of assisting: Remember our formula: Leadership + Management + Strategic Support = Business Partnership. This level of skills development and expertise can be achieved by hard work, study, and an active self-development strategy on the part of the Executive Assistant in order to yield talent that must be apparent.

If you have hired the Assistant who (1) is engaged in your work, (2) knows your company's business criteria, (3) knows what drives your decisions, (4) knows your triggers and sources of stress, (5) knows your areas of responsibilities and for what you will be held accountable, (6) knows how to incorporate his/her work into your and your company's mosaic, and (7) is "able to see around corners" and prepare for the worst, then pay that person well, provide expanding challenges within the role, and support educational opportunities to enable this Assistant to evolve.

For those Executives who are skeptical about this level of collaboration and partnership reliance, pretend you are on an Executive Outward Bound course, and that this is the only person on whom you must rely to get you through the most difficult challenges.

Executives Speak Out

In a one-day seminar for Executives on how to hire the best Executive Assistant, an Executive proceeded to define a top-level Assistant:

"An exemplary Executive Assistant is technology proficient, has common sense, and does not make mistakes in judgment. By that I mean that he/she has the ability to diagnose a situation, does not reveal information that should remain in confidence, has an understanding of boundaries, does not act outside of established procedures and policies, and does not argue a point of view.

"A terrific Assistant," he continued, "will remember that he/she gets paid to treat everyone well, and to make the day go as smoothly as possible, with a willingness to challenge ordinary thinking and the status quo. Selective flexibility is unacceptable."

Executive Assistants Speak Out

Even or especially in the more mundane aspects of the position, Executive Assistants will have the opportunity to assert those Emotional Intelligence skills that will guide the Executive Assistant to success.

"My employer asks me the same thing 500 times, and each time, I act as if it's the first time he has asked the question. I work for someone who will be unhappy even in Heaven."

A Vision for This Role

If the goal is to become more skillful in reducing superficial complexity to simplicity, to recognize how to get it right, and how to think the right way, how do you get there? You need a career-development strategy.

As with every profession, those who perform in this role will face an unprecedented level of difficulty in trying to keep up. Functional knowledge in global business, critical thinking, leadership and management are becoming basic requirements for filling this position. Ongoing education is essential and necessary for Assistants to be able to evolve strategically and to provide expertise in solving problems by placing facts in context and delivering them with impact, which requires fast response time and flexibility. Employers must invest in Executive Assistants by offering specialized, functional training and development the same way that they invest in all of the top-level talent in our high-performing organizations. It will not happen by chance. Any seasoned Executive will agree that inspiration and talent alone will only take you so far.

Expanding Executive Productivity: Intentions and Implications

Today, the tendency appears to be that of a progressive leaning toward higher and higher levels of responsibility, where certain tasks can be shifted from the Executive to the Executive Assistant. Any new approach to repositioning and redefining this team relationship comes with challenges. For these role transitions to be successful will require that (1) Executives focus on their Assistants' capabilities, (2) connect the tasks that can be assigned to the Assistant, and (3) provide key directional guidelines for these new, core activities.

The objective is to save Executives' time, maximize their effectiveness, and streamline processes and procedures. Not only is this a timesaving objective, but it is also a cost-efficient step. The most important thing to remember is that for Executives to be able to make these changes, it seems appropriate to assume that deciding what aspects of the Executive's role can be transferred to the Assistant (who must manage these new tasks with Executive-like confidence) would thereby free the Executive to assume other responsibilities.

Dramatic change is necessary to ensure there are shared interests, and that the process will be organized so as to decide which tactical challenge can be assigned early on, and which can be added as progress is achieved.

Executive Responsibility: Intentions and Implications

To advance your Assistant to the level of Business Partnership, there must be frequent interaction and communication and a well-thought-out process for the hand-off of work to your Assistant. Such a change would greatly improve workplace effectiveness and create new Executive Assistant opportunities. Among the most critical distinctions are the following seven steps that are to be considered in order to endorse your Assistant as a reliable Business Partner:

First: Remember that it will be necessary to challenge the Executive assisting role's historical value. The role's limitations are based on antiquated, underlying assumptions.

Second: Be knowledgeable about the skills and competence of your Assistant. Make sure that there is a vibrancy and sense of connectedness. Is this person qualified to handle a position that will steadily assume higher levels of responsibility? Does this person have the presence and interpersonal skills to counter doubts and demonstrate that he/she is well-prepared to assume the role? Does this individual have the capability, flexibility, and the right balance of skills to represent you to your top management team? Do you have the right person in the position?

Third: Match talents and skills to the tasks required. Confirm the pragmatist: the person who will not do something unless it is effective. Confirm competence and the ability to make suitable distinctions in decision-making.

Fourth: Outline your intention and confirm your expectations. There should be mutual agreement that this is an ongoing endeavor to ensure a Business Partnership relationship based on collaboration and coordinated and shared activities. To attract and retain the best and the brightest Assistant, challenge him/her with more to do of what it is that you do. This increases the return on your investment: so, set a high bar. Be sure your Assistant knows how you communicate (e-mail, in person, sit-down meetings, etc.). Know the management styles of the individuals your Assistant has supported in previous positions. Are they different than yours?

Fifth: You will increase your productivity if you demonstrate collaboration that will allow your Assistant to interact directly in order to gain specific experience and knowledge in the company's business. Broadcast to your team that your Assistant is assuming higher responsibility and will be included in key meetings; then get his/her input or new ideas. This will produce high motivation, achieve seamless coordination and capture new knowledge.

Sixth: Consider whether your choice of Executive Assistant will allow for these newly defined responsibilities to be assigned and effectively implemented. Make sure your Assistant is able to integrate and implement new knowledge. If not, identify the gaps in the must-have critical skills your strategy will require, then provide training and development opportunities.

Seventh: Consider management-level compensation for your Assistant. Going forward: remember that this is a deserved escalation. Your Executive Assistant is an accessible and reliable business resource who, when afforded the opportunity to master high-level assignments based on your judgment and discretion, will serve as a resource for Executive productivity improvement by freeing you from some responsibilities that can be redirected. This is a growth opportunity for Executives (who will have more time to seek out other opportunities) and Executive Assistants (who will accelerate activities with an informed strategy). If Assistants get to expand who they are, everybody gets to expand who they are.

Putting the Executive/Executive Assistant Team to Work: Recognizing and Awarding Superior Executive Assistant Performance

In order to appreciate the inroads made, it is necessary to put the Executive Assistant's accomplishments in some perspective. On a basic level, the Executive Assistant position, in the last 10 years, has steadily been redefined, and has attracted different validations. The characterization of the role has emerged while Assistants search for new ways to improve. Executives can, above all, grasp two very new facts: the acceptance, on the part of the Assistant, that this role has a renewed importance; and a renewed analysis of the relationships between the Executive and the Assistant. A series of positive facts are coming to form part of this transition, which is complex, though certainly not lacking in enthusiasm. The role is no longer symbolic; there is now a concentration on the function and its correlation at the level of partnership.

This new Executive/Executive Assistant course of action will advance capabilities at both levels. This will, of course, require that powerful Senior Executives meet the challenges of identifying and sharing their perspectives, being open to change and accepting the freedom to deviate from traditional perspectives that have defined this role. Senior Executives are in the unique position of being able to have a most positive influence on the Assistant. This suggests that a winning strategy will be achieved when Executives and their Assistants work together to solve problems, with information being freely imparted to the Assistant by the Executive. This will effectively transform the support role to one of Business Partnership.

Understanding Executive Assistant Superior Performance

Experienced Executive Assistants are perfectly positioned to drive business success, and to help Executives create their competitive advantage. Their talent is in their ability to take on Executives' concerns. These workplace contributors are tough-minded and can make emotionally difficult decisions. They bring moral passion to the position. These Assistants are filled with great, new ideas, and are comfortable with experimentation to achieve the end goal. These are individuals who should be encouraged to try different approaches, thereby helping Executives to realize more value-creating strategies. The key is to create a shared business strategy to achieve mutual success. No longer would predictable advancement be attributed to the Executive Assistant; this would be an earned escalation in the role. Our next work is to define this level of Executive Assistant responsibility through appropriate title and compensation.

The most seasoned Assistant brings very special capabilities; yet he/she can be one of the most under-utilized employees unless Executives are willing to accommodate a genuine expansion in the role's ascension. These are individuals who can produce high-quality work, given the opportunity to do so. It will be to all Executives' and companies' business advantage to not set limits on the transfer of challenging tasks to Executive Assistants. This requires that Executives put as much energy and intelligence into the *delegation* of tasks, and thereby reveal an enthusiastic *climate of engagement* with new processes and important advances. This is a new workplace progression that will ultimately free up Executives' time, while it allows for Executive Assistant growth and development.

This will be an important new step in forging the best partnership relationship, where there is mutual respect and an ethical commitment to each other's future success. Such a relationship provides a winning business opportunity that is based on core values of partnership, integrity, and personal responsibility. The idea is that more can be achieved by focusing on accountability and responsibility. Executive Assistants have worked within the constraints imposed on them. They are ready to accept the challenge of Executive-designed position descriptions. The reality is that changes in role content, attitude and levels of functioning will offer valuable professional experience for those Assistants who distinguish themselves as business-partner-ready.

When you think about the Executive/Executive Assistant team, its historical value is always placed within the context of the competent Assistant who strikes the right balance in managing day-to-day activities, and whose skilled decision-making reflects and responds to precise understanding of expected and unexpected events. Now, the key is for Executive Assistants to learn what aspects of the Executive's role they can assume and step forward to assume those responsibilities. Executives also must step forward to provide the opportunity for business-partner-ready Assistants.

How Executive Assistants Can Expand Their Influence

Take anxiety out of the Executive's day and manage to the Executive's business goals. Understanding the personal and business context of the Executive – within which he/she must manage the day-to-day responsibilities of the role – will make the Executive's life easier.

- Keep the Executive informed, and abreast of situations he/she would not focus on while doing his/her job.
- Have the courage to tell the Executive what you think... "Yes, but here's the problem."
- Treat small and big tasks with equal importance.
- Think through actions before taking them and consider the consequences.
- State what you are going to do and meet set expectations.

- Turn goals into an action plan with agreed-upon timelines; then execute.

Bear in mind that the Assistant's network of developed business friendships is an important aspect of the Executive and Assistant Business Partnership and serves as an invaluable resource. How Assistants think, act, and interrelate with people enables them to save the Executive time; managing and maintaining positive business relationships is key.

- Use available resources first to solve problems before seeking additional resources or asking for others' assistance. Confidentiality reigns.
- Maintain an even attitude and consistent tone of voice with everyone, anywhere, under any circumstances.
- Work together for the overall success of the group.
- Listen more than you talk; get needed information from people to keep the flow going.
- Avoid shortcuts, finger-pointing, blaming, or putting down co-workers.
- Pick up another's slack when it will benefit the whole.
- Avoid complaining, even when others are complaining around you.
- Use your sense of humor to offset setbacks.
- Tell all of the truth – without exceptions.

Executive Assistants are in control of their attitude. This allows them to choose a perspective that fits the situation.

It enables the Assistant to operate from a place that is most effective for the circumstances and the people involved. Obstacles and problems only serve as fuel for solutions.

- Work with the temperament and work habits of the Executive, and the needs of the organization.
- Be open and willing to change; be specific and take responsibility for outcomes.
- Follow up. Develop the ability to shape conversation: "The follow-up items we need to discuss this morning are…"
- Follow through. Ensure that objectives are met: "Okay…this is where we are now; I'll put myself on your calendar for tomorrow afternoon so we can close these open items on time."
- Never be satisfied with the status quo; strive for the optimal way of doing things.

Consider what the recent trajectory of business suggests about the future of the Executive/Executive Assistant team. Executive Assistants play an influential role in increasing the productivity of Executives. Assistants' capacity to function as both specialist and generalist allows them to apply sound judgment when responding to all circumstances and relieves Executives from some of the day-to-day crises. Executives will benefit from Assistants who have developed the traits, skills and capabilities that will get the job done well and present a positive window into the Executive's office.

- Appreciate employer(s) goals and pressures; respond accordingly.

- Focus on results; maximize efficiency; utilize technology to manage information flow, storage and retrieval.
- Weed through ambiguity; analyze developments; zero in on the most important points; keep Executive(s) informed.
- Build global interpersonal relationships.
- Monitor important concerns with others in the company – office politics are inevitable; the Assistant who is skilled in conflict resolution can ward off or ease circumstances before they reach the Executive.
- Stay ahead of the pertinent issues by providing new ideas and new research on relevant topics. Armed with summarized data, the Executive is aided in his/her decision-making process.

Remember: Executive Assistants' talents and skills enable people to be more productive. Productivity is enhanced when, by serving as a catalyst, the Assistant is able to insightfully navigate any predictable or unpredictable events, as they occur. Managing to the moment, moving from one event to another, on behalf of the Executive requires full knowledge of what the Executive's job is, and the context in which it supports the needs of the organization. This specialized decision-making ability provides a time advantage for the Executive, reduces setbacks, and helps to reduce interpersonal errors.

Cultivate the ability to understand the politics of the situation. Effective decision-making requires that you think like the Executive; see the business as a whole; know and understand the Executive; watch him/ her in action, observe non-verbal reactions. The great Assistant provides real value when he/she knows what the Executive values, then structures the way he/she works accordingly. The great Assistant can see what the Executive is thinking and is therefore able to do internally for the company what the Executive does externally for the company.

Remain committed to learning to do things better. Executive Assistants are vital to Executives as they show constant improvement – they know more and can do more, they learn from mistakes (theirs and others'), and as a result, they are able to make better decisions and exercise better judgments.

Every Assistant must be working on a personal development plan. What specific capabilities will the job require over the next few years? Contemporary job descriptions require new learning, which include:

- Keen understanding of economic trends and global events
- The importance of government regulations on business.
- General business and industry knowledge.
- Leadership and management.

Performing with this degree of learning and skill inspires and motivates, and it reflects a managed attitude of confidence, self-assurance, and continuous improvement. These traits allow Executive Assistants to consummately represent Executives and deal with anyone, anywhere, under any circumstances. C-Suite Executives themselves want to discuss details with confident, learned individuals; secure and savvy Assistants influence the entire team.

Without question, this role requires essential new learning. Mobility in this role must be maintained or Assistants will face an opportunity deficit. There is a need to prepare Executive Assistants for a new, complex economic and competitive environment. You need a broad understanding of how business works, and you need a broad understanding of how Executives think.

Sixty-Second Leadership©

"Hello. Did you arrive on time?" the Assistant asks of her employer.

"Yes, I see that you arranged for the family to be in the car to save us time…and for the sandwiches. I see that you also arranged to have the prep material for Monday morning's meeting."

"I thought that lunch in the car would be fun, " she explains, "and would keep the kids calm while you reviewed the contents of the file, allowing you a bit more free time over the weekend."

"Yes; one thing, though, next time, no mayonnaise."

"Ok", she responds. "By the way", she asks, "do you know Jean de La Bruyère's famous quote?"

"No," the Executive replies.

"'*There is no excess in the world so commendable as excessive gratitude.*' See you on Monday morning."

A short while later, she receives a call. "Hello?"

"I just called back to say 'thank you'," says the Executive.

"You're welcome…" responds the Assistant.

EQ/IQ *Case Story 2:* The Emotionally Intelligent Assistant: Leading with Urgency

"What do you mean the car is out of service?!" Naveen asks incredulously into her phone. Pausing from the work on her laptop, she begins to organize the emerging chaos.

It's 8:10 a.m. She's been at the office since 7 a.m. and has fifty minutes to finish the pitch deck. The Board of Investors is arriving at 9:30 a.m., and the Chairman of the Board is about to land at DTW expecting transport. Naveen, Scott, and the rest of the product development team have been preparing for this day for six months, and she's not going to let a cracked radiator throw it off course. She has been playing this day over in her mind, visualizing the company, herself included, successfully pitching to the Board their innovative solution to hands-free mobile purchasing using automotive VIN integration. The product and its corresponding subscription service will be disruptive to banking in the true sense of the word and if all goes well, the Board will be pleased.

Naveen tells the driver on the phone to cancel the pickup. A quick text to the VP's Assistant confirms her new plan is taking shape. She will send security to pick up the Chairman using the VPs fresh-off-the-lot black SUV; the Chairman will never know the difference.

Returning to her laptop, she again starts the process of reviewing the deck for formatting errors: *Slide 4 of 30 needs a line break correc*— her cell rings. It's Scott. He's in his office having trouble with his desktop. IT is unavailable, held up in the boardroom adding last minute changes to the demo. Naveen knows exactly what is wrong. She spent her first months as Scott's Executive Assistant learning the ins and outs of the business, impending department objectives and deadlines, and his distinctive, long rider of likes and dislikes. Evenings at home, on the other hand, were spent educating herself in finance, marketing, and consumer value indices, and, of course, common occurrence IT troubleshooting. "I'll be right there," she assures him.

Thirty minutes later Naveen is back at her desk. "Hello, Slide 4. Did you miss me?"

Powering through the deck, she wraps by 9:02 a.m. *Quite good considering the unexpected challenges of the morning*, she tells herself, recalling that self-control, initiative, and adaptability are useful competencies retaining her emotional intelligence toolkit.

The Takeaway. Emotionally intelligent Executive Assistants have the tenacity to make their emotions work for them rather than against them.

The Toolkit. Building on the concept of self-talk, the emotionally intelligent Executive Assistant uses moments of urgency, like the instances above, to rouse an opportunity discovery. This development espouses not only an awareness of emotional urgency but also the self-management of that emotional response, leading to resiliency and adaptability – two tenets of optimism. Resiliency, in this case, is Naveen's ability to embrace and rework challenges, maintaining a high level of performance, whereas adaptability enables her to pivot and adjust course quickly when urgency calls, making her emotions work for her. In doing so, the emotionally intelligent EA can

In doing so, the emotionally intelligent EA can neutra-lize stress and curtail burnout.

The Application. Manage your emotions: Synchronize your self-talk with optimism.

- Visualize yourself succeeding.
- Be proactive, not reactive.
- View challenges and changes as your allies, not your adversaries.

We know from experience that the C-suite is an environment that can shift from moment to moment, and its rapidly changing nature can subvert our best efforts to predict and plan for what is best described as unpredictable and unplanned. We've developed unique preparedness strategies to withstand change and survive sudden crises with robustness, but this case-by-case stomping of embers before they become a blaze cannot be sustained long-term. This is the danger of relying on robustness to combat crises. Which is why, for the good of the enterprise, the team, and the Executive/EA partnership, the new EA preparedness mindset requires not an episodic call to action, but a continuous revisiting of executive support strategy improvements led by the emotionally intelligent EA and expressed in their work response.

When we choose resilience over robustness, we are recovering from change by adapting to it. The Red Queen dilemma, coined by the University of Chicago in a nod to Lewis Carroll's *Through the Looking Glass*, describes a very tired Alice who, at the direction of Red Queen Iracebeth, has exhausted all her best efforts to run as fast as possible in a race against time and survival, because she finds herself unchanged in her advancements and running in place. This is our dilemma to solve if we merely concentrate on withstanding change: We are forced to keep running in place just to maintain our current position while the competition whirls forward and passes us by.

Executive assistants are capable of tremendous growth under pressure, even as point-in-time crises constantly reset his or her path forward. The good challenge, for many, will be to maintain that impelling force by drawing on the Emotional Intelligence skillset to bring out our strengths in having resiliency, flexibility, and making effective judgement calls to discover new opportunities, and adapt to crises in a way that propels us forward.

CHAPTER VII

Management, Leadership and Innovation

Global Executives who travel 80% of the time say they are "more prepared for life." What about those who prepare them to travel, so they can be more prepared for life? Let's begin. There are two basic aspects to the Executive/Executive Assistant Business Partnership that can be compared to two sides of the same door. The first aspect is that Executives and Assistants each confront complexity in responding swiftly to the changes affecting their organizations that require consistent focus and deliberate action. The second aspect is that each role values self-knowledge, personal strength and empowerment, as much as the ability to meet head-on the changes in global business and technology transitions.

For Executives and Assistants to compete on so many similar levels requires "smart power" and "common sense power." Your access to these competing considerations is creative leadership, innovation, operating dexterity, strategic competence, and global interpersonal skills.

Stability and vicarious on-the-job learning have brought the Executive Management Assistant career to its present status. Planning extensive global travel, with its complexity of multiple time zones, locations and cultures; responding to the impact of the Internet that adds a 24/7/365 urgency, which is defined by TTWA (Throw The Watch Away); and, holding down the fort during Executives' absence are fundamental to the position.

It is in this context that I give the content of the role of the Executive Assistant closer scrutiny for all it can mean to Executives and Assistants in their places of business. This is an age where we must get more specific. It is no longer just a matter of recovering a genuine understanding of the assisting role and trying to adapt these standards to a modern situation. This would be a false equivalence to what is now the centrality of the role.

Across all industries, there are two ways to describe this progression. One is where Executive Assistants *bring* innovation as they cope with change, *deliver* structure through the management of day-to-day routines, and *provide* Executive support by identifying and evaluating solutions to achieve common goals.

The other way is through proper recognition of this role as a *collaborative Business Partnership*, empowered with higher levels of responsibility and decision-making discretion. Those who serve as the liaison to Executives, and layers of the company, and who manage world-wide relationships, are essential contributors of influence.

This expansion process has given this role the credibility it has so often lacked. Cycling between old practices and new ones, in order to keep up with the driving forces of the future, Assistants are now faced with a crisis of competence, while work shifts from clerical to strategic support, and from manager to leader.

By now a question may be on your mind: What is the purpose of all this? This new role is a measurable standard because of its direct impact on Executive productivity. These skills are distinct from traditional skills, and the distinction is valid. In current experience, traditional and new skills weave themselves in and out of one another to become the whole, new position. This is the new and serious business of the effective Executive Assistant.

Understand that the successful application of these diverse and growing skills, and their capacity to maximize the Assistant as an agent of support, hinges on the Executive Assistant fulfilling his/her role as a competent and sensible ethical leader. Interacting and managing on behalf of the Executive demands that Assistants exercise good judgment, common sense power, and leadership instinct. Intimate understanding of the Executive's role and how it relates to the success of the organization is critical; with it, Assistants are empowered to operate on a level that matches the Executive – and as a business partner, this is exactly how they should perform.

What Outcomes Measure Success?

Anticipating your questions and your concerns, I have created an overview of the central role, with performance priorities:

Remember that in this continually evolving role, you bring the indispensable skills of leadership and management, and function as strategic support specialist, communication expert, technology expert, and Business Partner.

Remember what we established as the mark of a true leader: Character is your #1 attribute. Your personal style, professional judgment, self-management and compassion actually define your character. You cope with change, tolerate chaos, and inspire others with great passion to offer your best efforts on behalf of a goal to which you and the Executive are personally committed. Leadership is not about position or skill. It is about attitude. The truth is that the best leaders desire to support others, not themselves. Executive Assistants possess the confidence to skillfully provide support to others.

Assuming a leader's role presents a prime opportunity to shape the organization through the support you provide. The commitment and attention you invest in this regard determine your response to a multi-cultural, multi-generational workforce. Effective leadership will calibrate expectations among all staff members regardless of tenure or experience, bridge the communication gap between veteran and novice staff, and pave the way to a collaborative work effort. This is a social mission that informs the work that you do.

Of course, true leadership demonstrates the foresight and flexibility necessary to engender change. A mind that is open and active will preemptively search for solutions and set the strategies capable of achieving them. This approach permeates through all aspects of an Assistant's role, from daily events to future endeavors. Anticipating and adapting to change exemplifies your level of self-assurance. Confidence, conviction, stability and consistency are among your leadership principles.

As Manager, you generate the most complex reports by performing analyses on results. You organize and establish plans from ad hoc and specific objectives. You have an acute sensitivity for the vital importance of time urgency, exceptional follow-through skills, laser-like intensity, admirable people skills and wonderfully engaging styles and personalities. You communicate with Executives on key priorities, decisions and action items. You are able to see the big picture yet track operational minutiae. Assuming the manager's role means that the Assistant is the reminder and the supporter to balance today's pressure and longer-term accomplishments.

As Communication Expert, you serve as liaison, translate key messages, ask the right questions and listen well. Communication is key to all relationships. With clear, honest, timely communications, misunderstandings and false expectations are eliminated. Schedules are clarified. Personal preferences are explained. Compromises are worked out.

As Technology Expert, you work in a world that is massively interconnected. It is said that every thirteen months there is a doubling of information in the world. Executive Assistants process and analyze an enormous amount of data. You are spontaneously reinventing systems and processes to adapt your technological skills to create and manage time-saving solutions. You are systems-focused and systems-structured; you put the pieces together to move across boundaries. Executives prize technologically adept support professionals who perform with flawless execution.

As Business Partner, you are strong business allies, with a real share in the purpose and mission of the organization. You see the pure outline of things but understand the nuance. You understand: the Executive's role, goals and personal mission; your role in the company and in partnering with the Executive for performance; your boundaries and areas of responsibility; the lines of communication, formal and informal. The Executive/ Executive Assistant Business Partnership is the reward for the right "fit" between the Executive and his/her Assistant. Your intellectual and technical capabilities are vital aspects of the role; yet you remember that the "personality fit factor" sustains continued performance, both personally and organizationally. Mutual expectations must be established through open communication for a successful collegial relationship to develop. Influence is not shared; it is earned.

As Support Specialist, the key to Indispensability is your strategic support strategy. You accept that you have a constantly changing job description; you execute efficiently with relentless attention to details; and you maintain balance in your working partnerships. You work independently and as a team player; you take initiative and manage multiple tasks, relationships and projects where appropriate. Let me give you an example. Here's a client's description: "the ideal candidate must be a grammarian, possess the ability to think a situation through, and be able to shift gears in a nanosecond, while retaining complete composure." Consider the following:

You intercept a telephone call from the Executive stating that the car service is not on site; he needs to be at the airport for an outbound flight and traffic is heavy. At the same time, he receives an incoming e-mail from one of his many affiliations citing the need for an immediate Board of Director approval which requires his signature; furthermore, you receive another urgent telephone call for him. While this is happening, a critical press release comes across your desk containing an inaccurate fact about him as well as a grammatical error, and there are funds that need to be wired to one of his accounts.

In order to make this position work, you need to comprehend and instantaneously prioritize these events in real time and confidently take action. This requires patience, focus and good problem-solving brain power. Here is where you push the boundaries of the role, testing its limits.

Achieving the perfect working relationship is based on the principle that Executives have the hidden expectation that their Assistants will be empathetic and charitable; likewise, Executive Assistants have the hidden expectation that they will be valued by the Executives they support. This involves knowing each other's strengths and supporting each other in areas for development. Interpretation is almost everything. Each is expected to learn from the other's experiences, understand the other's role, personal mission, demands and pressures, blind spots, work habits, and temperament. Says Sam Levenson, famous American humorist and author, "You must learn from the mistakes of others. You can't possibly live long enough to make them all yourself."

An effective course of action requires Corporate responsibility, Executive responsibility and Executive Assistant responsibility. Let's respond to the following questions: Who are we as Executives, Corporate Leaders, Entrepreneurs? Who are we as Executive Assistants?

Corporate Responsibility. Companies must put into place compensation systems that align with contribution and commitment, invest in education (the quality of the workforce matters), hire the right people for the position and assure job clarity. This role must be given great prominence.

There is a tendency among many who hire to estimate a person's aptitude for this position by his/her skills and recognizably good judgment. These are predictable aspects of a successful profile but are unpredictable as to outcome. Because someone appears to have these talents, that does not mean they have the inclination to do this work. Satisfaction in this position is realized by helping someone else to be successful. The importance of the role is that there is great value in being a strong right hand.

Executive Responsibility: Start with talented people, lay out the rules, communicate, motivate and reward your Assistant. If you do all those things effectively, "you can't miss", says Lee Iacocca. To reinvigorate that thought, consider what steps you need to take. Here's an idea to consider: today, it is now more widely recognized, although not absolutely accepted, that the only way to keep organizations vital is to instill in individuals at all levels a sense of initiative, opportunity and responsibility.

Executive Assistant Responsibility: The future of the Executive Assistant rests upon courses of study that emphasize practical knowledge for a broader perspective. The goal should be to acquire hard and soft skills so as to be familiar with the theories of finance and economics, operations, marketing, financial analysis, management, project planning, strategic decision-making, areas of management theory, the international political and financial system, the impact of government regulation on business, and familiarity with the dynamics and differences of organization cultures.

Those who are preoccupied about the future know that navigating for enduring success in the workplace requires new learning. Work rules have changed; people are not measured by intention; rather they are assessed by their ability to adapt to changing circumstances, their enthusiasm to learn new personal behaviors and workplace skills, by their decisions that sustain successful outcomes, and by their belief in the value of contribution and commitment as a basic tenet of their professional values.

You play a central role in supporting Executives' efforts to manage the extraordinary transitions that await all of us in the coming years; so, make capabilities the main pillar of your strategy. Invest in your education.

You excel in this career because you enjoy the self-management focus, the opportunity for collegial decision-making, new learning, and recognition for your participation in corporate achievements. The evolving role of the Executive Assistant is more integral to the realization of management goals than ever before. It is a workplace integration and evolution that will continue. The Executive Support position continues to be a smart career option, with a rewarding future.

Those who think they can leap to this level of skill without pursuing new learning, deceive themselves. This is a legitimate concern. Consider that we do not take occasional swimmers and enter them into an Ironman event. The downside is that you are either wading in water, or swimming full speed ahead.

If you just think you *may* want to be an Assistant—don't. If you are inclined to do this work, and *need* to be a professional Assistant, be prepared to face the ever-changing and growth-demands of the position. For those who are inclined to walk the tight rope, this role is pretty irresistible.

The process I have laid out should yield a lot of promising initiatives and a portfolio of actions with a short- and long-term focus. I can't reassure you or make up an answer for you. You are experts in establishing priorities; so, the choice is yours!

I grant you that's a lot on your plate. Yet, you and I know that there are no "impossible things" for Executive Assistants. Like the Queen in Alice in Wonderland, we not only believe in them before breakfast; we find a way to make them possible before dinner.

The combined role of the professional Executive Assistant requires strength of character, empathy, detail accuracy, global communication skills, initiative and a sense of humor. The Executive Assistant position driven by process innovation and multi-disciplinary learning is Indispensable. These skills are embodied within the art of assisting and underscore the essential assets I categorize as Indispensable in any business environment. My message to

Executive Assistants is to take charge of your career. Your position is valuable and important. Don't be confined by your job description. Be the one to expand it.

Finding ways to remain flexible and persistent to adapt to the changes we encounter as a result of the impact of economic uncertainty, technological transformation, a multi-generational/cultural workforce, growing globalization and innovation is the current imperative. Those who provide management support will face their greatest test of authenticity: the viability of the role. Consider a professional development agenda to gain a better understanding, and to expand within your role.

Sixty-Second Leadership©

Social-Awareness: Trust your gut. As you let go and listen to an individual or a group, sometimes a clear impression or intuitive response will surface out of the listening. Trust that. Consider offering your observation. Be brief, gentle, and clear and ask for a response from them about your observation.

Self-Manage: Anticipate stress. Know your tendency to get triggered in a particular situation or with a particular person and be on your guard. Be clear what outcome you want, prepare questions to ask and formulate your responses to their anticipated questions. Keep emotional upset at arm's length. Put on your helmet.

EQ / IQ

CHAPTER VIII

Here's the Light Switch!
The Executive Assistant's Role in Driving High Performance

I am here to articulate the Executive Assistant's role in the world, and to emphasize your critical importance to the corporate structure of our economy. I have spent over 15 years as a Senior Assistant and Chief of Staff to CEOs, and over 30 years recruiting and placing C-Suite Executive Assistants in the most diverse and powerful offices of top companies, domestically and internationally.

Only those of us who have been challenged as we aimed to be near-perfect Assistants truly love and understand the complexity of the role. So much of what is encountered and managed every day cannot be expressed in a standard job description. I know from personal experience that the intrigue of this field is that you never have a boring day, and that you must relish that part, and the stress that comes with it.

So, where are *you* in the role? What are the required skills and characteristics of the Near-Perfect Executive Assistant?

Let's acknowledge that you are Near-Perfect Executive Assistants, working for very busy Executives who depend upon you to manage their business and personal lives. Do you own your position? Are you dedicated to the Executive you support, your company and your peers? Are you detail-oriented? Do you anticipate problems before they occur, and do you know what Executives need before they know it themselves? Do you maintain your own personal life, which is equally important as your career? How would you answer these questions?

Are you like my best friend, Laurie, who works for a busy Executive who depends upon her to manage all aspects of his business goals, his relationship to the business and the planned and unplanned occurrences in his private life? She works 12-14-hour days. She works on weekends; if not physically in the office, then her cell phone and laptop are on all the time, and she receives calls throughout the weekend with questions and requests.

She expands her role to accommodate the needs of the Executive's family. Her office routine includes managing calls, sorting through 100+ e-mails daily (she handles about 50%), establishing priorities for day-to-day activities, monitoring follow-up items, navigating the flow of communication, managing special projects, prioritizing calendar commitments, coordinating and confirming complex meetings. She reviews mail, follows up on requests, gathers briefing material for meetings and trips. She supports the Executive on projects.

Her relationship is rooted in partnership and friendship. Even when he runs the marathon, she has her phone programmed with the numbers of his friends who are along the route, to alert them to have his water or energy drinks ready. On Monday morning, she sends the thank you notes. She makes certain all bases are covered. She is compulsive about details; she works from task lists with confirmed dates, following up every assignment to completion. She turns in daily status reports.

Travel, meetings, and itineraries are all handled to the minutest detail. This requires that she checks weather conditions (for proper clothing), and secures the right seat on the aircraft, and arranges for his favorite food to be served on board if he is traveling on private aircraft. Hotel room dimensions are confirmed. Breakfast is ordered and delivered to the room at the right time. She follows up with the hotel to ensure this takes place. For meetings: she arranges for ground transportation, with name of the driver, make of the car, license plate number and waiting location confirmed – and reconfirmed. She has the contact information for participants in every meeting including: clients' home number (especially if it's an early morning meeting), their wives' and children's names (to help him with his social skills), clients' cell numbers, their Assistants' names and numbers, in case there is a last minute change.

All this information is included in the itinerary, and programmed into his iPhone; but, Laurie always knows to expect a call - sometimes it's about the one detail she missed (and she makes a note to include this the next time). She follows up to make sure all meetings are confirmed, she double-checks flights and departure times. She makes sure he is in the car and on the way to the airport when he is supposed to be. Planning for his return, Laurie calls, texts, or e-mails (or all three!) to remind him that his driver will meet him at the baggage claim to take him to his dinner meeting.

Everyone prefers coming to her for help, advice, and direction. She persuades and influences. She is always willing to help, and others are also willing to help her. If she needs to step away from her desk (some of us do), she has a team member who is conversant with all the details to manage in her absence. She is the Ambassador. Laurie knows as much (if not more) about computer software than her IT person. She tracks ideas on the Internet for current background information to keep her Executive apprised. She monitors trends in technology. She does her best to remove or take care of potential obstacles in advance. She makes decisions, takes action and takes responsibility for whatever happens. She has stretched beyond the formal boundaries of the position. She makes time for herself, family and friends. She brings balance to her life! She does not neglect her own needs!

All these work habits eliminate frustration: saves time, gets the Executive to the right place, with the right information, and on schedule. Laurie knows that there can be no shortcuts, which can lead to costly errors in judgment.

It is very hard to figure out what the fundamental value of something is. I offer that this level of detail management, which incorporates planning for contingencies, and allows the Executive to operate at peak efficiency, impacts the company's bottom line. In the simplest terms, what I have suggested as the business value for the Near-Perfect Assistant role is that:

- Your goal is excellence.
- You take responsibility.
- You are open to critique.
- You do it all with a smile.
- You do it for the satisfaction of doing it, regardless of the degree of recognition you receive.
- You do it because it helps someone else to be great.

Is this how you manage your role? If so, what special gifts, talents and expertise do you possess that enable you to seamlessly handle the myriad responsibilities of such a complex position? Two of our greatest gifts are imagination and humor. Imagination compensates for what we are not; humor compensates for what we are!

You deal with a variety of people, cultures, situations, problems, decisions, and technologies. In essence, you have to know how to coordinate an enormous mass of detail to keep both the life of the person you are working with and your organization running as smoothly as possible. And, as we all know, this isn't easy in an atmosphere that can sometimes resemble a circus.

In this ring, ladies and gentlemen, are the ERTs (Endlessly Ringing Telephones), in that ring are the CWTs (Clock-Watching Temps) and over there are the INCEO (Incompetent Nephews of the CEO). You are in the center ring, in the midst of it all. You are the main attraction, the IOS… (Island of Stability)!

Yes, Executive Assistant life is very much like a circus, and no performance on any given day will be quite like the one the day before. I'll bet we have all had times where we have thought something like, "Just shoot me out of the cannon now, and be done with it." But you persevere, meeting every challenge, learning new skills, and broadening your talents and inner resources so that you become the star attraction, if not the ringmaster. You are the main attraction because you are skilled in mastering relationships that are successfully based on proper fit.

Here are the "The 7 Commandments of the Competent, Near-Perfect Executive Assistant."

1. Provide the Executive with the support to achieve his/her best.

2. Accept the conditions and requirements of the support role. (i.e., you sit on your emotions; this is the price you pay for this position. I don't know if that's good, but it is necessary.)

3. Cultivate a solid, trusting, respectful relationship through openness, consistence, honesty and humor.

4. Be responsible and accountable for your performance.

5. Perform with quiet diligence. Acknowledge that passion and discipline are your greatest assets. Vince Lombardi, legendary football coach, tells us that "Mental toughness is many things and rather difficult to explain. Its qualities are sacrifice and self-denial. Also, most importantly, it is combined with a perfectly disciplined will that refuses to give in. It's a state of mind – you could call it character in action."

6. Do more than is expected.
7. Balance upsets or mistakes with apology and humor. Nobody cares how much you know until they know how much you care! Are you where you want to be? If not, how do you get there?

Here's the light switch!

This position is defined more by your attitude, tenacity and commitment to the role. Make sure you and the Executive you support have the right fit, share mutual goals, communicate openly and like each other. Manage yourself first! Self-management is the source of your personal power. It forces you to squarely confront your own limitations and motives, and to accept the challenge of working to improve your own qualities to surpass yourself and others.

Excellence is your motivation, which always comes back to defining your goals, to achieving those goals, and to making that achievement a sufficient reward. Excellence is the tangible result of the quality of your relationship. Excellence is going back to the basics: understanding your Executive; knowing what he or she values; understanding his or her work needs and acting on this understanding. Any time you fully comprehend something or someone, you can better deal with it or them. When the fit is perfect, you are like-minded, and you can readily answer the following questions: How does your Executive like to have things happen? How would he/she approach this? What does he/she think would work best in certain situations? How does he/she deal with disappointments, pressure, mistakes?

Now, where, exactly, do you fit into the organization? How do you help your company to maximize its competitive advantage?

Here's the light switch!

Two things determine the quality of your life: the things you say and the people around you. So, change your language to create a positive reality. You know that your Executive is not mercurial or cruel or indifferent. He/she is focused, driven, committed. You are a partner in your Executive's success. You are the ultimate team player. Negative thoughts and emotions destroy our experience of peace and undermine our health. You are optimistic when the chips are down. You prowl the horizon for creative solutions, sure that they are out there somewhere. You are vigilant. You do not think of a mistake as a failure. You think of it as a "time-release" success. You do not take yourself too seriously. Where a novice Assistant might let a mistake fluster him/her and send him/her into fits of apologies, as a near-perfect Assistant, you know that a good chuckle and a wave of the hand can save the day. You know when to laugh at yourself.

Here is a moment that comes to mind: Linda is a very efficient Executive Assistant who lives in Connecticut. She makes few mistakes. Usually, nothing flusters her. One day, Linda was waiting in line at a local ice cream shop, with Paul Newman right behind her. He lives in the area and it was not uncommon to see him in the local shops and markets.

Linda noticed him immediately, although she pretended not to. Now, there is an unspoken rule in the town that the locals do not pester him or treat him differently. Plus, she is not the kind of person who fawns over celebrities! She is used to dealing with high profile people! But she really wanted his autograph…*really* wanted his autograph. Still, she resisted; tapped into her *professional discipline*, and purchased her cone – in the most casual way possible – and left the store. Moments later, she swept back into the ice cream parlor, admittedly a bit flustered. She stepped up to the counter. Mr. Newman nodded for her to step in front of him. "I am sorry. I forgot to take my ice cream," she said to the clerk behind the counter. "Ma'am, I gave you the ice cream," the puzzled clerk answered.

Linda was just as puzzled and was about to explain to him that he did not, in fact, give her the ice cream when Mr. Newman stepped up quietly and said, "Excuse me, Ma'am, I believe you put the ice cream in your purse…along with your change." True story! Even the most competent among us sometimes do not handle ourselves as well as we would like, in our private lives or our business lives. But you are tenacious! You keep going…even when you are cleaning Cherry Garcia out of your handbag!

Your personal excellence is determined by how you rise to these not-so-perfect situations. I'm sure one of you out there is thinking, "But, Melba, what happens when I have exhausted every creative solution?" There is no end to creative thinking when inspired by a positive attitude.

Here's the light switch!

Be creative *and* street-smart. Being creative enables you to look at an environment, turn it upside down and inside out, and see things in new ways --to relate, reclassify, rearrange, and restructure your approach to the existing circumstances. Being street-smart enables you to know how to read the situation, determine what is needed to succeed, and adapt your thinking and behavior so as to succeed in that environment.

How does what you do impact the people you work with, and the company overall? Executive success and the company's success are directly connected to your ability to meet the challenge of managing different personalities, getting them on the same page – while achieving expected results. You manage and facilitate every minute of every day – from the most mundane act to the most strategic assignment. And that makes you indispensable. Although somewhat behind the scenes, you are the person engaged at many levels. If you are the right person in the right job, you are in the spotlight for solving problems. Otherwise, simply put, if you look the part but do not have the substance, qualities or skills to effectively do the job, your presence jeopardizes the integrity of your office and those around you. Everyone notices your effectiveness or lack thereof. Either way, you impact the bottom line. What are you expected to do and how are you expected to do it?

Here's the light switch!

Avoid the pitfalls. Let loss of control of your work habits be your foremost concern. The biggest hurdle in the work of the Executive Assistant is planning for the unexpected. Undetected errors in relatively simple-sounding tasks can have serious consequences. Some direct mistakes are easily corrected; more "subtle-carry-forward" errors point the finger back at you. You are expected to make the right things happen at the right time. You are expected to provide a predictable path of doing things no one else did or perhaps wanted to do, and you are expected to achieve the desired and sometimes unanticipated results.

You might think of yourself as the master juggler – and rightly so! On any given day, you will be called upon to juggle any number of balls, keeping them all in the air at one time with such adroitness that none may fall.

Some of the balls you will be able to handle easily. Others will be tossed at you out of nowhere, forcing you to adjust your routine mid-stream. But that isn't all: in addition to being a juggler, you also have that high wire balancing act to maintain. In fact, you are often doing both acts at the same time! Meeting expectations equals high risk.

Your ability to meet deadlines will make it possible to achieve goals. Your skill at keeping an Executive fully informed will enable him or her to make intelligent decisions. Your expertise in a particular software application will ensure that output is timely and accurate, and information is stored and accessible at the moment. Your willingness to hone your skills to meet organizational needs keeps you well-balanced and helps you to keep all of those balls in the air. As you already know, managing deadlines, communication strategy, and technology also equals high risk.

It can all be rather mind-boggling, yes? Yet in the midst of the chaos, there is a sense of celebration. Each demand that is made on your time and attention is a chance to celebrate as you work to make order out of chaos.

Another moment for celebration of a miracle is when someone walks over to your desk and says, "You are doing an incredible job. I don't know what I would do without you!" You know that your good work, your personal sacrifice – all of it will largely go unacknowledged. You may forever be under-appreciated – and not get the accolades you deserve! "Above-and-beyond" is a regular day at the office for you and most days I will bet that no one notices.

You are expected to provide your own validation. It means that you know who you are and what you contribute. It means that you take care of yourself. You acknowledge yourself. You pat yourself on the back and seek out your own rewards. You have to – because no one else will do it for you.

Own your position and celebrate tasks well done through self-recognition and self-validation. Self-validation is important because you are out there working with a full spectrum of personalities!

Here's the light switch!

Here are Thirteen High Risk Commandments that help avoid the pitfalls:

- Confirm "what needs to be done," then do it.
- Develop action plans and execute.
- Follow up to completion.

- Take responsibility for your decisions; be accountable.
- Focus on opportunities rather than problems.
- Find out what's needed for a situation and when and provide it.
- Know that attention to detail is your most vital skill.
- Listen first; speak last.
- Communicate so that you are understood.
- Get the knowledge you need.
- Think and say "we" rather than "I".
- Be a supportive member of the team: serve as a Mentor – lead others to your level.
- Learn what is best for the Executive, colleagues, and the company – and meet those needs.

Near-perfect Executive Assistants have patience, diplomatic and social skills, unrivaled clarity, compulsive detail management, and get the right things done, and on time. You know you are doing a great job because while doing exemplary work, your diligence to constantly improve by acquiring new skills, and your willingness to manage and lead, have earned you the status of Managers and Leaders.

You set your own self-development objectives. You know that for success and longevity, improvement is required in awareness, common sense, and technical expertise. And in many ways, you are the CEO of your Executive's life! That is how important you are to the vibrancy of the company. Make no mistake and let no one tell you differently: you keep your company running. You have a stake in its future and a role in its growth. How you manage your Executive's life directly influences how he/she manages the life of the company. By my standards, that makes you integral to the success of your company.

You lead by example, manage people and routines, and serve as an ambassador for the Executive and your company. These roles will definitely test your mettle. Yet you do not over-compensate; you are authentically yourself and you rely on all the terrific skills that qualify you as managers and leaders. You have the ability to solve problems that even your Executive can't solve. That is your job.

You create an environment that imposes order on chaos or looks for order in chaos. You inspire; you are not thrown by tense moments, rather, you move and bend with it. You accept ambiguity. You are a tall oak standing still and straight and strong, while the wind whips and beats around you!

"Gathering chaos into a satisfying order is a daunting challenge," says Twyla Tharp in her book, The Creative Habit. "There are a number of possibilities, but only one solution looks inevitable." You know that indecision is the access to your flexibility.

You take great ideas from staff meetings and vanguard strategies from the boardroom, and *you* give them legs. You make the ideas real. You execute for the visionaries. You handle from the mundane to the strategic, without a pause. You manage distractions. You create the context for your role and develop the content.

The near-perfect Executive Assistant has developed strong "situation sensors," a middle-ground between intuition and information. With it, you can sniff out the signals in the environment and sense what's going on without having anything spelled out for you. You can read those subtle, non-verbal clues. You can accurately judge whether relationships are working or not. This is a complex process; the results are impressive.

With this degree of tact and sensitivity, it is no surprise that you keep confidences. You are privy to sensitive data and insights. Some of these tasks require knowledge and experience. But most require a sense of judgement, confidence and the trust that comes with another critical quality that I emphasize – your integrity. Your unswerving sense of honesty and discretion is called upon daily.

You allow your decisions to be based on ethical principles. You act out of concern for others' well-being. In a word, you live ethically. In "Ethical Ambition", Derrick Bell defines "ethical living" as "an ongoing commitment, as we meet life's day-to-day challenges and opportunities, to assume risk in honor of self and all others." In other words, to be ethical is an act of courage. And the purpose of being ethical is to honor one's self.

You are a hard-nosed enforcer and empathic peace officer. You are a Queen or King and a foot soldier, and you glide between these two roles with grace and ease. You give everyone a chance, and do not take anyone else's word for another's behavior – you learn for yourself.

You have self-control. You are flexible, open to change and you respond in the moment. You are present – one eye on the future, but "right there," minute to minute. You are loyal and committed to inspiring people around you. You know that, as Shakespeare wrote, "the past is prologue". You live in the present.

My hope for you is that you know what I know – that you make a difference; that you make a contribution; that you have the power to create change that not only impacts the people around you, but will ripple effect in ways you cannot possibly imagine; that your influence transforms the workplace!

And mostly, I hope you know that through your service, you achieve greatness every day. You are great. You do great things. You are the esteemed tradition of excellence! It is in your power to influence and improve the whole dynamic of your position. By your grace, wit, aplomb and skills, what might have seemed unattainable or not worth the trouble, can become your moment to shine: to influence!

Advanced skills are required in this ever-evolving global economy. Executives face unmet needs as they struggle to find skilled individuals in key positions of essential administrative support, whose primary job is to add real value with the ability to bring creativity (move from the old way of doing things to the new), adaptation to change (bigger government and heavier regulation), global and business knowledge, along with the advanced technology transitions to meet their requirements. The focus is on improved productivity, institutional effectiveness, innovative solutions to societal, global and economic trends, and technological transitions. We need action and progressive vision to bridge gaps wherever they adversely impact our effectiveness, rather than a hope that members of this workplace sector will simply persevere.

Sixty-Second Leadership©

Empathize. Sympathy is feeling *for* someone. Empathy is feeling *with* someone. Empathy means that you relate with the emotion of another and that you express that in some way: "That can't feel good." "Wow, that seems overwhelming."

Empathy is about connecting to the feelings of someone else because you connect to those feelings in yourself. It requires some vulnerability. Most often, when someone tells us something that is painful, we want to fix it, offer advice or diminish its importance. Those may be all good impulses but often people do not want to be fixed or have someone talk them out of their feelings. They just want to be heard. Empathy is listening at a deep level.

Social Awareness: Give them your attention. Put away distractions, turn down your inner dialogue, let go and be with the other person. Avoid judgment, labeling and reactivity. "Get" their emotion, sense their intention and try to hear what is being communicated beyond their words.

EQ/IQ *Case Story 3*: **Leading as Thought Partner**

Outside was white. A heavy layer of fog pressed against the windows, playing with the light. It was later in the day than the sky suggested. Facing the window, Scott was taking a break from his open binder. He hadn't noticed the usually thriving office had quieted down for the day. The stillness of the fog mirrored the mood indoors.

"Managing people is a lot different than building what they need," he said into a furled hand. He often sat like this when deep in thought. It has been a long week balancing responsibility with creativity and freedom. Shutting the binder, he swiveled his chair around and stopped to face Naveen.

"Is *this* the last of them?" he said half-jokingly, holding up the binder.

"*Yes,*" Naveen answered with equal emphasis. Standing up, she took the binder and added it to the pile with the others just like it.

"These org charts and yearly projections make my eyes swim."

"I know," she agreed. "It's a lot. But after the weekend, you'll be ready for Boston."

On Monday, Scott would depart Detroit to visit the East Coast office. Leadership suggested that he make the trip in person his first week as Chief Creative Officer, a promotion that was well-earned and a long-time coming. This week, the week before his transition, felt like a crash course in telecommunications: Wake up, calls before breakfast, calls during his drive to work, calls from the parking lot to his desk, calls all morning, followed by an afternoon and evening of calls. He was on the phone so frequently that he had no time to download the pertinent information with Naveen.

"Naveen, I almost forgot," Scott said as he packed the binders into his travel case, "I need to change my departure time because…"

"Because you're meeting with the Vice President on Monday at 8 a.m. for breakfast," she said with confidence. "I chose a spot on the way to the airport."

Scott turned to look at Naveen.

"When you were busy with calls, I went through the call list on our linked computers. You gave me access; I figured now was the best time to use it. I connected with your contacts' Executive Assistants, and they gave me the rundown of changes."

"That's… that's great. Thanks," he said with a satisfied smile.

"I also bumped Tuesday's mid-day meeting request with Boston's Director of Sales and the regional buyer to Wednesday for dinner. Your first, full day is packed, and I figured you'd want some built-in time on Tuesday to get to know the team in Boston before meeting with external parties."

"Perfect. I hadn't even told you about that meeting request yet."

"I know," she said. "I called Boston and they told me."

"I'm so glad that you knew to do this."

"Your success is my success, Scott," Naveen said lightly.

"And, apparently, your success is mine," he replied, folding his arms and leaning back in his chair. He turned to face the window, catching the last light of day. The fog had lifted.

The Takeaway. Establishing a Thought Partnership is a pivotal, transformational process that occurs within the relationship between the Executive Assistant and the Executive, which develops over time. Formed within the space of creativity, confidentiality, and commonality, the Thought Partner is less of an advisor and more of strategic business partner that challenges the Executive's thinking schemes with positive intent.

The initial steps of the partnership are a series of trust-building moments, where the Executive Assistant and Executive establish specific communicable boundaries within their prescribed roles. A Thought Partnership occurs when the Executive and Executive Assistant recognize that "Aha" moment in which they acknowledge the collaborative value of each other's contribution to both their working relationship and to the enterprise.

The Toolkit. Employ the Four CARE Building blocks:

- **Communication**: Demonstrate commitment via confidential communication; engage in truthful, forward-moving conversations with shared purpose, social receptibility, and good intent.

- **Acceptance:** Be vulnerable, warts and all; thus, you will be accepted. Build a common understanding.

- **Reliability:** Establish reliability via reciprocal knowledge sharing.

- **Empathy:** offer an actionable point of view, grounded in the acknowledgement of another's concern.

The Application. Approach every conversation from a long-term, partnership-building mindset. Practice active listening to fine tune your sounding board abilities. Demonstrate that you understand the Executive's universe by providing reliable, actionable feedback designed to maximize their time, and your effort.

EQ / IQ

CHAPTER IX

In A Nutshell:
A Summarized View

#1.   *Today, attitudes toward the role have changed dramatically.*
      While the Executive Assistant's role will continue to be
      defined in relation to the Executive's responsibilities
      and the structure and culture of the organization, in
      this dynamically-evolving economy, the work of the
      Executive Assistant is placed squarely in the middle
      of the work of the Executive. This is an opportunity
      for the Executive/Executive Assistant Business
      Partnership to exceed past accomplishments and enter
      new territory by incorporating different renditions of
      the role of Assistant. This level of skills development
      and expertise can be achieved by hard work, study,
      and an active self-development strategy on the part
      of the Executive Assistant in order to yield talent that
      must be apparent.

#2.   *The success of an Assistant is in part related to the
      Executive's ability to trust, delegate, and clearly
      communicate.* In my work, we have questions that
      are designed to elicit the attitude, perception, and
      management style of the Executive. The answers
      to these questions are the basis of assessing "fit."

True Business Partnerships rely on the right skills and personality "fit", entail mutual trust, superior communication and the elusive element of give-and-take. Smart Assistants pay attention to clues in the Executive's behavior and shifts in temperament, because timing and judgment are the foundation of a smooth working relationship. Developing an effective working relationship requires that you know the Executive's needs, strengths, areas for improvement, triggers and personal style. Smart Executives pay attention to the same clues in their Assistants. This creates a mutual advantage for achieving success.

#3. *Executives*: If you have hired the Assistant who (1) is engaged in your work, (2) knows your company's business criteria, (3) knows what drives your decisions, (4) knows your triggers and sources of stress, (5) knows your areas of responsibilities and for what you will be held accountable, (6) knows how to incorporate his/her work into your and your company's mosaic, and (7) is "able to see around corners" and prepare for the worst, then pay that person well, make available expanding challenges in his/her areas of responsibility, offer decision-making authority, and provide educational opportunities to enable this valuable colleague to achieve satisfaction by expanding within the role.

#4. *Executive's needs:* In a one-day seminar for Executives on "how to hire the right Executive Assistant", I heard the following remarks: "To ensure our productivity, I want speed and accuracy. If I can't get both, I will take accuracy. Speed translates to competitive advantage;

mistakes do not." Another: "I need an Assistant who can deal with various levels of patience if he/she doesn't get it right". Another: "What's happened to basic job skills, punctuality, reliability, flexibility and proper dress?"

One Executive from the rear raised his hand and proceeded to define a top-level Assistant: "A spectacular Assistant," he said, "is able to read my mind, displace my concern, engage with me in constant dialogue to create a new collective perspective, understand the unpredictable nature of my work, is always learning new ways to improve on what we have to get done, understands that a computer only answers questions, it does not ask them." Another Executive succinctly stated: "The attributes I am looking for in an Executive Assistant are the ability to withstand adversity, to admit mistakes, to manage his/her emotions, and to manage spousal interface."

And it was at that very seminar where I heard from the Executive quoted in Chapter VI, whose idea of an "exemplary Executive Assistant" accurately orients the Assistant's sights on meeting an Executive's needs: "technology proficient, has common sense, street smarts, and does not make mistakes in judgment"; someone who is able to "diagnose a situation" and "not reveal information that should remain in confidence;" who understands and respects policies, procedures and boundaries; an individual who is open and adaptable because he/she knows that "selective flexibility" is unsustainable. "A terrific Assistant will remember that he/she gets paid to treat everyone well, and to make the day go as smoothly as possible, with a willingness to challenge ordinary thinking and the status quo." In summary, the expert Assistant focuses on the consequence of the task and how he/she can add value.

#5. *The effective organization recognizes that the competencies Executive Assistants need are changing dramatically.* The emerging Executive Assistant role blends talent with skill and education. Those in this position are not just business-savvy, they are business-educated, leveraging an informed understanding of business, communication, and technology in their approach and contributions. Where their disposition guides their response to personalities and circumstances, their education informs their analysis and decision-making. These qualities make them the perfect partner to work confidentially with Executives, as the modern Assistant can skillfully handle critical information and ideas with sensitivity and ingenuity. They can seamlessly integrate the new with the existing, and create the most efficient version: analysis; priority; execution. Professional Executive Assistants are innovative and equipped to perform beyond the old standard, as much out of personal investment as of necessity. The globalized climate of the business market demands an individual who is educated, informed, quick on their feet, highly skilled, and intuitive. The next phase of Executive Assistant meets those expectations and is prepared to meet the demands of the future.

#6. *As Executives face the growing pressures of competitiveness, they will of necessity drive creativity and innovation at the Executive Assistant level.* The effective Assistant possesses the right skillset and the right mindset to handle authority and decision-making as an extension of the Executive's intention. Executives will no doubt turn to their Assistants more and more for their communication, ingenuity, corporate investment, and personal commitment to everyone's success. Trusted and valued Assistants will flourish as reliably autonomous partners, called upon to lead as much as they support.

Smart Executives realize that they need to clone themselves, and it is experienced Assistants' ability to "think like an Executive" that places them firmly in the co-pilot's seat. No Executive can be everywhere or do everything at once; an intimate understanding of Executive responsibility, both business and personal, allows Assistants to provide the support that alleviates this stress and anxiety. Assistants whose methods and objectives align with both the big picture and day-to-day goals of their Executives prove to be the best people to help "fly the plane."

#7. *A business education program targeted to the Executive Assistant level is necessary to permit growth solutions in this role.* I urge companies and Executives to motivate their Assistants with career development strategies. This is the mission of the Duncan Leadership Institute curriculum. It responds to questions asked by business leaders who animate around the issues of: How do we get our staff motivated? How do we get our staff to learn new skills in order to maintain our competitiveness?

In my experience, breakdowns in Executive/ Executive Assistant Business Partnerships mostly occur when Assistants are not learning and applying new skills, are not consistently prepared to offer techniques and great ideas that are of the most value, and are not encouraged to deliver the highest levels of performance. Active, continuous education remains an imperative in all professions in order to effectively manage increasing amounts of data and computer power – the role of the Executive Assistant is no exception. Employers must invest in Executive Assistant development the same way that they invest in all of their top-level talent in our high-performing organizations. It will not happen by chance. Inspiration only goes so far. Executives need to play a key role in advancing educational opportunities for their staff; many seem to ignore or shy away from this responsibility.

#8. *There is an extraordinary community of talented Executive Assistants at work today.* With unprecedented skill, talented Executive Assistants bring administrative stability with effectiveness and efficiency, with the discipline to handle more, and manage the magnitude of systems with consistency and reliability. Executive success is dependent upon this level of support provided by these talented individuals, whose purpose is to focus on goal accomplishment to meet the needs of Executives and the companies they support. Executives who hire the best Assistants, yet who fail to capitalize on the most obvious resource sitting a few yards away from their desk hampers Assistants' effectiveness and stifles their career advancement.

#9. *For the hiring Executive:* Although most of your focus when choosing an Assistant will be on appearance and social skill impressions, there are some important practical concerns to be considered as well. Obviously, you will need to make sure that important details are spelled out before, not after, the Assistant begins employment. Conversations should be specific to the position and should be discussed up front to assure that both parties agree on requirements and expectations. If it feels like you might have trouble working together, take heed. But if all goes well, and it feels like a good fit, ask for references – and do not neglect to personally make the calls. You want to know about the Assistant's work habits and communication style. You want to know about this candidate's unique disposition and capacities. Be sure you like what you hear. The wrong person is depleting, versus energizing; this can be a tragic misadventure. Remember that resumes tell us how we were prepared to do the last work, not how we will do the next.

#10. *Professional Executive Assistants know that a 9-5 frame of mind is a serious liability in times of change when expectations management is critical.* Executives, I offer a scenario that bears repeating: Imagine that your Assistant is someone who you may have to call in the middle of the night with an idea or a task that you urgently need executed first thing in the morning. Then, upon your arrival the next morning, you are greeted by this person (who had arrived at the crack of dawn) with the reassurance that the task has been handled; that the most effective course of action (that works with your calendar and relieves you of multiple conversations on the same topic) was to have arranged a video-conference call so that you can communicate your idea to your global marketing team. This is the person who enables you to meet the challenges of the global business landscape. This is the person whose strategic decisions save you and others' time. This person's unquestionable value is in the ability to perform as your daily, minute-by-minute responder/problem-solver.

#11. In my *Harvard Business Review* article, "The Case for Executive Assistants", I wrote that *in some ways, an Executive's ability to leverage the skills of his/her Assistant is a good measure of certain aspects of his/her leadership profile.* Can the Executive trust and delegate? Is he/she a micro-manager? Do Assistants like working for him/her, or does he/she have a record of many Assistants leaving or being fired? Not every Executive/Executive Assistant business relationship is made in Heaven! But an Executive's ability to manage conflict with his/her Assistant may well be a "referendum" on his/her ability to manage people more generally. Business leaders can see the full potential for the Executive/Executive Assistant dynamic and utilize the experience to learn the nuanced art of delegation and managing complicated relationships and workflow.

#12. *It will take a concerted effort to go about resetting goals and preparing people, and the business setting itself, for this expanding Executive/Executive Assistant Business Partnership.* Endeavoring to reposition the role of the Executive Assistant requires the important connection of planning, focus and intention. There is no single agreed-upon description of what the position entails, or even what the appropriate title should be. The position is structurally, strategically, socially and politically unique and extraordinarily situational. Professionalizing the role, then, will require standardization of skills at all levels.

#13. *Advanced skills are required in the new economy.* The business world is changing. Adapting to these changes, in many ways, requires continuous professional development. Executives are hard-pressed to find individuals who are able to contribute more than just the traditional skills of an Assistant. Executive Assistants must understand that the essence of their value is in their willingness to meet change head-on, and creatively apply their skills and education. Examine the old and embrace the new in the interest of finding *what works best.* Keep current with changing trends in business, global expansion and regulation so that you are strategically prepared to respond quickly and meaningfully.

Stay informed, technically, and technologically – education is the surest road to success in any arena. Lastly, invest yourself in who you are, what you do, and with whom you work. Appreciate diversity on a global scale and within the company and be confident in your own merit and contributions. Having professional courage will aid your efforts to innovate and strengthen the support you provide.

EQ / IQ

CHAPTER X

Executive and Executive Assistant Comportment: How Hard Is It to Be Successful? The Bar Just Got Higher.

There's a point I would like to make, right here, right now: I am referring to the act of Executive bullying of those individuals who help them to achieve and retain success, and for whom there is no safety net. It is said that personality is divided into two parts: temperament, and character. To get to this matter, I would like to take this opportunity to talk about three very important elements in the Executive/ Executive Assistant business relationship that are almost totally overlooked.

If I were to say to you that one of the great characteristics of assisting is detail accuracy, I am sure you would agree. But there is another aspect to assisting, just as central, just as essential as detail accuracy. It is right here that we come to the core of the Executive-Executive Assistant business relationship: Humanity. Humanity is an integral part of assisting that must be treated with seriousness and appreciation, and can only be made evident through *mutual respect*, *trust*, and *reliable friendship*. Without these three elements there is no real relationship, no real Business Partnership. Without these human qualities there can be no real success, no sense of accomplishment, no sense of working together as a team for each to achieve success.

Here is why I bring this up. People in power sometimes do as they choose to do and continue to do so even if there are well-chronicled deficiencies. Some behaviors are overt, and some methods are more subtle, and perhaps less destructive; yet we should recognize these actions for what they intend. Executive Assistants who are subject to the whims of Executives behaving in unpredictable ways pay a huge price. Talented, self-confident Executive Assistants know the importance of trust and respect. When you think about it, the Assistant's ability to sustain composure and focus while some Executives (and sometimes their families) behave in a demeaning manner is remarkable.

Career Assistants who remain strong in this role, yet who are subjected to these circumstances, do not succumb to learned helplessness: they know how to take a provocation pause. But occasionally they do need psychological boosting. A place to start is to establish and keep to your boundaries of how you want to be treated.

Where I remain confident in these circumstances is that Assistants possess self-knowledge, self-leadership, and self-management. These are imperatives. Most important is that they know their predisposition to independence or dependence on authority figures. They know that we are continuously shaped by our experience, and that it is our outlook that confers value on those experiences.

The Executive is in charge and the Assistant knows it. Of critical significance is that if you are facing workplace challenges it is important to realize that (1) we can't "fix" people; and (2) our self-esteem is reinforced when we are in environments that reconfirm our contribution and our value. If the Executive you support has total disregard for your welfare, make sure you are not a complicit responder; rather, be an advocate for your own well-being. Speak up.

Executive Assistant Comportment

Here's another point I would like to make, right here, right now: I know that there are some Assistants who speak negatively about the Executive(s) they support, or who transfer their frustration to their team members either by emulating Executive behavior, or assuming the power and authority of the Executive in getting things done. If you are among those who pass along to your team (or others) the tension of your business relationship, or if your style and manner is problematic, perhaps it is time to re-evaluate your intention. Remember (1) that when it comes right down to it, our reputation and influence are all that we have; and (2) respect is a universal language, and it is free.

Road Map for Professional Assistants' Future

The Executive/Executive Assistant Business Partnership is a dynamic that is critically important to the success of any organization, in which everybody has a stake: The Executive, the Executive Assistant and the enterprise. This is the Executive Assistant's competitive edge!

You are the next-phase Assistants who will fill the talent gap through the processes of ingenuity, concentration, analysis, communication, time management and decision-making. You are the individuals who work confidentially with Executives. As such, you are subject to the same demands and changes at all levels of influence: business, personal, technology, and time. New initiatives or insights are thrown your way with the expectation that you have the skills to catch the pass and run the ball to the end zone. You cannot allow any obstacle to get in your way, even if another ball is thrown to you, mid-run. But remember, the ball is in your hands for a reason. You are trusted for your ability to handle every pass, for your grace under pressure, your quick and accurate decisions, your flexibility, adaptability, and intuition.

These are precise specifications for the professional Executive Assistant as a collaborative Business Partner. Together, these elements reinforce the creative quality of this position. I realize that is a remarkable job description; yet you are poised to be a remarkable contributor. You are constantly changing, and unfailingly working toward finding the right balance in your working partnerships, while at the same time finding new ways to execute at full efficiency.

Much of what I have described here has to do with repositioning this role. An Assistant may assume he/she is doing a good job; but will not know that for sure without agreed-upon expectations, establishing clarity of direction, and determining and confirming goals and objectives with the Executive.

Getting Personal

We now know the details of your strategy for outstanding performance. But our journey isn't quite over. Let's look now at the personal assets that make performance possible in the first place. These include your experience (what you have done; how much you have expanded within this position) and your competencies (what you are capable of: the art of innovation).

Most Important are the 3Hs: Personal Honor, Intellectual Humility, and Awareness of Humanity

Here are some everyday examples of a lack of respect for others; a lack of personal honor, which is defined as an act contrary to what you feel you should do for another:

Think about a time you felt you should apologize to someone, but never got around to doing it. Or a time when you knew you had some information that would be helpful to a co-worker, but you kept it to yourself. Or maybe a time when you needed to stay late to finish an assignment for someone but instead went home without bothering to talk to anyone about it.

Perhaps we might alter this behavior by admitting that what we believe forms our perceptions and that our perceptions determine our actions. We could observe how we react to our mistakes. We could remember that the Executive Assistant's contribution is unique to her/his company's business and to the health and welfare of the Executive or teams she/he supports. Perhaps if we pursue the course of self-discovery, we will find that we have created a sense of personal worth or importance by comparing ourselves with others. It is possible, therefore, that we have a vested interest in the subtle inferiority of others.

We need to notice whether our actions reveal that we live in a world of closed options, set judgments, predetermined positions and guaranteed conclusions that leave us little room for "others." A lack of personal Honor!

Perhaps we instead focus on results. Perhaps we don't try to be perfect; we try to be better. Perhaps we worry less about whether others are helping us and embrace helping others.

Intellectual Humility

Who you are, your vision, your character, and your priorities are all attributes of your attitude and personality. Self-awareness and knowledge shape how these attributes are expressed and applied for the better. Understanding the extent of what you know and your passion for ongoing learning and improvement is evidence of your Intellectual Humility. You are aware of the talents you offer; you do not pretend or claim to know more or to be able to do more than your skills and experience allow. You do not brag; you listen to others and you are respectful. You have respect for the knowledge and talents of others, you are open minded and can work towards the best solutions as a member of the team. What is key is that you know that you do not know everything; thus, you are open to new learning and respectful of others' knowledge and experience. When we are operating at peak performance levels, we bring all these assets to bear, and we are "world-beaters."

Awareness of Humanity

When we are not at our best, we create problems that diminish the value of all that productive energy. We may just go down in flames, and perhaps drag our co-workers, and our organizations, down with us. In my work as a Coach and Consultant for Support Staff, I observe that while companies are focusing on global competitiveness, employees are sometimes engaged in workplace drama that can demoralize the team's effectiveness.

One particularly tantalizing thought that I discovered in *Leadership and Self Deception*, published by the Arbinger Institute, is the problem of Self-Betrayal/Self-Deception. Acknowledged as an important idea in organizational thinking, Self-Betrayal is defined by the author as the "germ that creates the disease of Self-Deception." To help ensure that your career path will be long and rewarding, I challenge you to recognize your own habitual performance deficits. Keep in mind that it is said that personality is divided into two parts: temperament and character.

For an in-depth discussion of this Self-Betrayal/Self-Deception behavioral dynamic, I recommend a cover-to-cover reading of this important book. In particular, I point to the Institute's theory that self-deception can be so pervasive that it actually determines one's experience in every aspect of life. I believe that self-deception plays a major role in our current and best explanations of the difficulty we have, at times, with building and maintaining healthy workplace environments. The Arbinger study points out that self-deception, also called "resistance", undermines successful performance, both our own and others'. It keeps us from seeing how we can be part of the root cause of much of the problems that impede organizational performance, including problems relating to leadership, teamwork, communication, accountability, trust, commitment, and motivation.

Being self-deceived means that we inflate others' faults, inflate our own virtue, inflate the value of things that justify our actions, and we attach blame. We drift farther from the human element of our interactions by creating villains and heroes through blame and subjectivity. And we pull others into our way of being by justifying our actions, through our gossip communication skills and body language.

This behavior is easier to fall into than we might imagine. With very little effort, we can become infectiously self-deceptive and demoralizing to ourselves, our colleagues, and our organizations. We must strive not to be the person whose blind spot becomes a flaw, or whose "derailer" activities become development needs. This is clearly the wrong direction. We are successful only if we are learning how we can be more helpful to others.

Just to give you a sense of how this could influence your actions, the next time you slip into the 'blame' space, ask yourself what you have contributed to this action. If discomfort begins and you want to move away from that feeling by justifying, you are stepping into the self-betrayal space. Stay in the discomfort until you see the other person as needing just what you need.

Remember, we act according to the way we perceive things, and that perception is not fact. To impose our perception on others renders them invisible. How do you fix it if you don't look at it?

Let me highlight a key element of the solution: do not focus on what others are doing wrong; focus on what you can do right to help. Be open to this as a possibility. Let's agree to adopt this as the simplest perspective and imagine that all the steps are fundamental to ensure the distinguishing characteristics of the Executive Assistant.

In my communication with Administrative support teams, I sometimes find that there is reluctance to accept the theoretical assertion that there can be a destructive power operating within these support teams that is facilitated by Executive/Executive Assistant relationships, and that is allowed to remain unchecked because it is misunderstood and not addressed as a group concern. This process makes it almost impossible for companies to develop a healthy pattern of organizational ecology. The consequences of such benign neglect can keep companies in creative destruction, while experiencing excessive turnover, poor performance or marginal enthusiasm for the success of the business.

The circumstantial evidence I have in mind here relies on the fact that we are fundamentally capable of these behaviors. Once we accept this, our work really begins. The truth matters. You make critical connections: who you know is as important as what you know. You build a rich, diverse network which enables you to gain access to information, solve problems collaboratively and achieve goals. You adjust your mind-set. You course correct. You figure out how the changes in your environment will affect what you're trying to achieve.

Remember that people with rich networks tend to solve problems faster and with better results. Be the person who knows "whom to call", the person who knows "what to do next", the person who energizes others, not the person who creates bottlenecks. Strengthen your collaborative capabilities. Much depends on what you know, and with whom you speak.

One last word as we contemplate our performance strategy: we've seen that change is a constant. Expand your responsibilities and demonstrate how much you can contribute to your organization. Stay informed. Support and motivate; bring the team together. Share new knowledge regarding best practices. Be prepared to take on more responsibility. Your organizations expect more of you personally and as a healthy contributor to your team, so, be ready to develop new skills and build on current ones. Be diligent. Cooperate. Integrate. Share knowledge. Finally, simplify! Trust Albert Einstein when he said, "Make things as simple as possible, but no simpler."

EQ/IQ Case Story 4: The Builder – Leading with Empathy

Emerging from the vestibule, Naveen looks to the open kitchen where Allie had texted she would be seated. Naveen spots her among the crowd. Seated alone at a high-top table, Allie waves to her boss from across the dining room. Allie has been working as Scott's Administrative Assistant for a year, enabling Naveen to step into her role as Senior Executive Assistant by taking over the bulk of key administrative responsibilities.

Under Scott's leadership, growth at Autov8 has been explosive; the company has ridden the edge of ingenuity to deliver to buyers what they all knew was possible. Now, that same growth was fueling the industry's growing curiosity for something new. Leadership, sensing that demand, was sending it downstream to the Creative Department – Naveen's department. The pressure was mounting for a technical breakthrough, and Naveen and Allie were meeting to discuss the future expansion of their team.

Naveen settles in across from Allie and the two catch up on the events of the day before placing their orders with the server. It's clear from any vantage point that the women like and respect one another; but Allie seems distracted during dinner, somewhat ridged. When dinner is finished and the plates are cleared, Naveen decides it's time to discuss what they have come together to consider.

"I appreciate your willingness to meet with me after work," Naveen starts. "First, I want to recognize how well you've been doing at Autov8. The speed at which you've learned the role and your advancement, it's a huge value add; you really are an integral part of this team."

"Thank you," Allie says, nodding her head in acknowledgement.

"You're welcome," Naveen continues. "Second, the e-mail that I sent you about Scott approving the promotion of a second Administrative Assistant; I would like to talk about that and the positive changes it will bring. Specifically, I would like to invite you to have a hand in the selection." Naveen finishes. She waits for Allie to say something, but she does not.

"Do you have any questions for me?" Naveen kindly prompts.

Choosing her words carefully, Allie begins: "I appreciate your assessment of my work and inviting me to have a voice in the selection process, but I have to ask, why are we adding a second assistant?"

"We are adding a second assistant because our department is expanding in line with Autov8's interdepartmental expansion. This addition will reinforce our commitment to balancing future pressure demands brought on by our expanding customer base. This is a very good thing; it will mean more opportunities for our team, and for you in particular, Allie," Naveen assures.

"I get that we are growing. Your e-mail was quite detailed, but I think I can handle this growth without having to share my job," Allie returns, her voice getting firmer. "And, if I may speak directly, I don't see how splitting my responsibilities with a second assistant can equate to more opportunities for me. If anything, it sounds like I'll be responsible for less."

Receiving her words, Naveen repeats what Allie has shared to ensure she hasn't missed anything. She agrees with Allie; Allie is expressly capable.

"This expansion will add to *your* experience," Naveen explains, "because it will allow for expanded learning and faster growth, providing the opportunity for you to stretch your competencies and adopt greater responsibilities.

"You'll be adopting a greater share of responsibilities, not less, and we want to run parallel to that by investing in your potential, both financially and developmentally. Your skills and future merit that investment, and we will have an updated agreement for you to review in the next couple of days. This agreement will not only highlight your pathway to success, it will redefine your role with your consent and input. So, are you interested and excited about taking on more with us?"

Allie draws a long breath and exhales her answer: "Yes." She hears Naveen and likes what she hears, and feels assured that Naveen has heard her... but she has to know – "Will the new promotion be my equal, my downline, or my upline?"

Naveen smiles, aware of the concerns and importance of career-path trajectory. Understanding the stream of meaning flowing between them, she says to Allie, "You'll both be point-persons, and together, you'll be our ears on the ground."

The Takeaway. The emotionally intelligent Executive Assistant sees relationship building, especially conflict, as an opportunity to generate the kinds of events that they want for a future that benefits the *other*, and the enterprise. In today's automated world, the need for human-driven competencies is more important than ever. Empathic and ethical considerations help navigate conflicts to a point of meaningful resolution. There is no substitute for the value this brings. Artificial intelligence, driven by algorithms, cannot innovate outside the parameters of the job in such an impactful way. Future-proofed by Emotional Intelligence, the Executive Assistant won't be threatened by algorithms; they will thrive.

The Toolkit. To overcome conflict, build consensus using Emotional Restoration, a utility within the Emotional Intelligence toolkit. Here's how:

- Define success in four terms: Conflict parties should openly and honestly share their interests – their *needs, wants, hesitations,* and *fears* – to gain a ground-level sense of the disconnect. Focusing on interests over conflicting sides or resources will help to reduce subconscious egos, thereby clearing the way for smoother, more fluid emotional restoration. This first phase is an exercise in self-awareness and self-management, two of four domains of Emotional Intelligence (EI).

- Increase buy-in, forming one large pie: Combine the conflict parties' interests. The second phase is not to be mistaken with compromise and splitting the difference, but rather a willingness to make tradeoffs in favor of achieving joint-value outcomes. This will enlarge the pie and, by default, cultivate 360°-participation and accountability. Those who are accountable will also be rewarded. Social awareness, the third domain of EI, will increase your ability to read the room, connect to Others' views, and expand the vision.

- Collaborate and then effectuate the plan: A) Emotional restoration solutions must be collaborative, transparent, and documented if they are to be effectual, as in no single party could have conceived of this solution. B) Final phase introduction, allocation of "the pie", is evidenced by the parties being in agreement, the roles being defined, and the groups having developed strategies for real change. C) Relationship building, the fourth domain of EI, supersedes the original conflict, and the *builders* of the relationship will implement the plan, maintaining stability by minding early interest gaps through regular feedback.

The Application. Everything is interconnected: Problems today are generally the product of solutions from yesterday; and so "solutionizing" must be new going forward. To better stay ahead of conflict or disruption, use emotional restoration to fuse individual interests into the work and restore balance to the system (the individual, the team, the organization); in doing so, we are opening new pathways to meet the challenge of the moment. This practice of re-architecting work and building human elements into everything we do will prioritize the organization's survival today and expansion tomorrow.

To restore balance to the system (the individual, the team, the organization), use emotional restoration, and remember: to offer genuine understanding and perceptual embodiments for the Other without any prosocial inclinations is to be deeply empathetic, a distinctively human and future-proof trademark. People will give their very best when they feel supported by leadership and their peers, and more likely to establish meaningful connections to the overarching goals of the enterprise.

CHAPTER XI

What Gets Us Where We Want to Be? The Executive Assistant's Powers of Work

The people in the ranks of top management have always had a list of things they can't do without help from a real, live human being: someone who, with tact and diplomacy, is a tenacious inquisitor to get the facts, and who knows virtually everything of consequence about the company for which he or she works. I would argue that this list is typically longer today than it was ten years ago, and that the Executive Assistant who helps manage this aforementioned list now is one of the most important players in the entire organization. The Executive Assistants' Powers of Work acknowledge these skillsets that support the expectations of Business Leaders.

Professional Executive Assistants, you represent a high business function. Your wealth of skills and depth of knowledge define you as a dependable asset to your Executive and company. And what best distinguishes the value of your talents is how you apply those skills. Let me again emphasize that the professional Executive Assistant role requires the use of your imagination as you encounter and manage the element of unexpectedness. Doing produces learning. The key is to welcome the challenge offered by change, while we find a way to integrate what we love into the work that we do. Professional Executive Assistants meet this challenge while they exemplify and exceed the following Powers of Work.

The Power of Continuous Professional Development

Executives will benefit from Assistants who have developed this new set of capabilities, in the areas of greatest importance to meet the challenges ahead. These skills combine traditional activities and introduce the ability to provide sophisticated business skills (management, leadership), with a high level of efficiency. Assistants will need to identify critical gaps in their capabilities, ensuring there is a foundation on which management teams can rely. Assistants will need to excel in these areas to tackle the challenges they face and be deliberate in their self-development goals so that they do not fall behind in their own expectations.

Companies must motivate their Assistants with career development strategies and offer recognition and training programs. We urge all companies to adopt such a policy, to build their teams from within by expanding the business skills of their existing Assistant teams.

The Power of Sharing Strategies for Applying Key Learnings

At a minimum, Executive Assistants appreciate Executives' goals and pressures, and areas for improvement.

They know the best time and the best manner to present information and to get approval for something they want to try. They always look at decisions made from the Executives' point of view. They build the relationship by focusing on the positive. They avoid engaging in the emotions of the moment; they state their concerns or differing opinions at a time when they will be heard.

The Power of Innovation

When we think of work, we only consider functions. Most of us put a great deal of time into work, not only because we must work, but because work is central to our well-being. We are crafting ourselves, individuating. Our work is an extension or reflection of ourselves. When we conclude a complex task successfully, we feel good about ourselves. If what we do is not up to our standards, if we allow ourselves to do substandard work, or if we are not prepared to meet the work requirements, our output does not reflect our attention and care. And when we stand back and look at it, we suffer. Work is a vocation: we are called to it. But we are also loved by our work. It can excite us, comfort us, and make us feel fulfilled.

The products of our work are like the image in a pond: a means of loving ourselves. When that inherent reflection is lost, we become more concerned instead with how our work reflects on our reputations. We are then tempted to find satisfaction in money, prestige and the trappings of success.

The Power of Professionalism

I am delighted that others agree with my thinking.

In *The Power of Professionalism,* author Bill Wiersma asks the question: "What does it really mean to be a professional?" He challenges conventional wisdom and asks us to think differently about whether it is your title or degree that makes you a professional. Bill Wiersma suggests, and I absolutely agree, that the mind-set concerning a professional reflects who a person is, not what a person does. The mind-set transcends temperament, social hierarchy, and intellectual prowess.

He describes professionals as an increasingly rare breed, often taking the proverbial road less traveled. They are not only smart; they are also wise. Their ability to exercise good judgments stands above the rest. Professionals willingly invest discretionary effort. They keep their wits under tough conditions and refuse to respond in kind when they are wronged. Their work is not necessarily about what they do, but rather how they do it. People who view themselves as professionals have higher morale, better job satisfaction, and more job longevity. A major point Wiersma makes is that "You don't need to pursue a traditional profession in order to be a professional, let alone demonstrate professionalism. Any individual desiring to hold the lofty mantle of professional can do so regardless of circumstances or background."

The Power of Self-Discipline

You cannot meet your goals and expectations without it. There are clear rules of behavior enforced by management and a strong sense of self-discipline imposed by higher performing, successful individuals. Self-discipline helps us to choose our behaviors and reactions, instead of being ruled by them.

The Power of Self-Awareness

This is the ability to work with the temperament, and work habits of Executives and to respond to your company's processes, procedures, and culture. You understand who you are and how you relate to people and circumstances. Your position requires Management and Leadership skills. The Power of Self-Awareness is necessary to improve upon those skills. The pursuit of intellectual and technical knowledge can be undertaken with excessive fervor and single-mindedness; however, we suffer when we are reduced to our functions. Without self-awareness, which is the underpinning of the state of well-being, we lose sight of who we are capable of becoming, especially in challenging circumstances, and how we impact others in all of our relationships. Self-awareness is vitally important to assess who we are, and to recognize emotional patterns in order to overcome obstacles, internal and external, and to reach our full potential.

You know the triggers and understand the needs and characteristics of the people with whom you work. This kind of understanding helps in planning, organization, and execution, which is getting the right things done, at the right time, with the right people. Assistants who are inclined to do this work respond with self-awareness and with situational appropriateness to subtle interpersonal cues. Self-awareness is the key to well-being. Self-awareness is the ability to read your own emotions and accurately align your personality to the circumstance.

The Power of Emotional Intelligence

This entails not simply picking up cues from other people and intuiting their motives but regulating one's own frustrations deftly enough to keep moving forward. To better illustrate this process, let us examine how the emotions that we feel when we experience satisfaction, ace a project, or lose a race, are triggered by our senses. Once triggered, our senses direct various impulses along a network of interconnected cells much like cars move along a network of connected highways. These stimuli travel at a rate of high speed straight to the brain's limbic system. This is why we feel before we think and act. Our brain is designed to process emotion before we process information and formulate decisions. The informed Executive Assistant understands this critical network of emotive and information processing and uses this baseline understanding to her/his advantage.

The Power of Self-Management/Personality Management

Self-management is a source of personal power that enables us to take control of our circumstances. It begins with a focus on the imperative of transforming anger into positive action. Self-awareness is the key; yet it is difficult to maintain our own emotional perspective. Pursuing knowledge in self-development, listening techniques, decision-making and conflict resolution techniques are strongly recommended. The key is to acquire the ability to separate the signal from the noise and to respond accordingly. Remember that to a hammer, everything is a nail; be open to changing your point of view because perception is not always fact.

You excel in this career because you enjoy the self-management focus, the opportunity for collegial decision-making, new learning, and recognition for your participation in corporate achievements. The evolving role of the Executive Assistant is more integral to the realization of management goals than ever before. It is a workplace integration and evolution that will continue.

Throughout my more than thirty years' experience in hiring and placing Executive Assistants there has emerged a professional class; that of Professional Executive Assistant. The influence of these individuals defends this "thesis" of integral involvement in every moment when the Executive shines. And, as with every profession, ongoing education remains necessary. Self-management keeps disruptive emotions under control. Our goal is to be trustworthy, flexible, and optimistic. Our goal is to expand within the role.

The Power of the Vital Skill of Empathy

"Everyone feels benevolent if nothing happens to be annoying him at the moment." – C. S. Lewis

Nothing reaches across the entire domain of Executive Assistant support as the vital skill of empathy. It is hard to make a credible claim of effective Executive management if you do not have the capability to demonstrate understanding and support with compassion and sensitivity. Empathy changes your thinking and changes your language.

Empathy is the sustaining essential skill for successful strategic support, management and leadership. It means you are aware of the feelings of others, and how it impacts their perception. It does not mean you have to agree with how they see things; rather being empathetic means you are willing and able to appreciate what the other person is experiencing.

Empathy requires nonjudgmental listening, openness and emotional intelligence. One key trait is the ability to listen attentively to those around you. Empathy is an important factor in relationships; it is positively related to job performance. To be able to lead, collaborate, across organizational and cultural boundaries, and create alignment and commitment with individuals who have different values and cultures requires empathy.

The Power of Trust

The element of Trust is especially important. Trust is critical, says Bill Wiersma, in his book, *The Power of Professionalism*: Trust is "the emotional glue that supports one's priorities, protects one's self-interests, and ensures respect for one's values." We learn from this essential book that the determining key is to leverage the resource closest to your desk and thereby increase the value you place on that relationship.

This means that Executives elevate the role of their Executive Assistant to the level of Business Partnership by recognizing and acknowledging strategic competence, by delegating higher levels of responsibility, and by apprising others in the enterprise that this is a trusted and knowledgeable colleague, whose job it is to efficiently expedite and manage to the needs of the moment.

The Power of Influence through Productivity and Effectiveness

Influence is essential! In healthy partnerships, successful performance is enhanced when Executives and Assistants possess real freedom and the social power to influence decisions. Influence means that you are involved in deciding how to accomplish your work goals. Intelligence and skillset are never the only parts of the equation. Longevity and success in any business partnership hinges on how well the partners mesh on a personal level. Remember that the "personality fit factor" determines the presence (or absence) of trust, respect, and room for levity and camaraderie in the face of changes and challenges.

The changing role of the Executive Assistant comes across clearly when looking at how Executive Management teams are most concerned with the efficiency and effectiveness of their organizations. Executive success is dependent upon the careful and strategic support offered by Professional Assistants as they respond to the needs of corporate America by their ability to focus on accomplishing agreed-upon goals.

The Power of Collaboration

The Power of Collaboration places the responsibility on Executives to keep their Assistants informed. Why? Because the aware and knowledgeable Executive Assistant does not allow the Executive's vision to transcend his/her capabilities. This is the genius of this role and the influence of a Collaborative Partnership.

Executives who communicate with honesty and candor enhance an Assistant's capability to expand and develop in the role. In collaborative business partnerships there is an implicit contract and commitment that requires a mutual exchange of ideas and appreciation for each other's point of view.

The Power of the Idea

"The Singularity is Near" by Ray Kurzweil is a story predicated on the idea that "We have the ability to understand our own intelligence; to access our own source code, and then revise and expand it." The author says that "No matter what quandaries we face – business problems, health issues, relationship difficulties, as well as great scientific, social and cultural challenges of our time, there is an idea that can help us to prevail. Furthermore, we can find that idea. And when we find it, we need to implement it. The Power of the Idea: this is itself an idea. Ideas prompt innovation and exist to solve most any problem that we encounter."

Sixty-Second Leadership©

"Hello. Is this Miss Sympatico?"

"Yes," I respond. "May I ask who is calling?"

"Yes, Ma'am. I am the taxi driver and I have a Mr. Enlightened in the back seat of my car. He insisted that I call and tell you that he is late for his flight and that you need to call the airlines and hold the plane."

"I don't believe I can do that, Sir," I reply. "Please ask Mr. Enlightened if he wants to take the next flight – it is listed on his itinerary."

"Please, Miss Sympatico, I am driving a taxi, and he just handed me a folder full of papers and asked me to find the itinerary and I can't do that and drive."

"Please put him on the phone... Hello, yes, you will have an extra hour at the airport if you miss your scheduled flight. You will need to go to the ticket counter to have your flight changed."

"Just call them and tell them to hold the plane," Mr. Enlightened interrupts. I remind him that although they will know that he needs to be on the flight, that because of present regulations, they will apologize but will not hold the flight. I hear the phone change hands again.

"Miss Sympatico? This is the taxi driver. He asked me to tell you that if I drive and get a ticket for going over the speed limit that I am to call you and let you know."

Please tell Mr. Enlightened that I understand. And I thank you.

EQ / IQ

CHAPTER XII

Roadblocks to Mastery

The following quote from Albert Einstein can cause a fair amount of debate:

"A human being is part of the whole called by us universe, a part limited in time and space. He experiences himself, his thoughts and feelings as something separated from the rest, a kind of optical delusion of his consciousness. This delusion is kind of a prison for us, restricting us to our personal desires and to affection for a few persons nearest to us. Our task must be to free ourselves from this prison by widening our circle of compassion to embrace all living creatures and the whole nature in its beauty."

Commentaries on this principle suggest that "we come to realize that we are nothing but interrelatedness, that we exist only in relation to the world, including other people, and that we have no separate existence in any real sense. We are completely and inseparably connected on a physical, mental, and emotional level with other beings."

This concept of interconnectedness is one with a profound connection to how we can view all that we do. It informs all levels of our interactions, business to personal. Furthermore, it shapes how we acknowledge and appreciate contributions from others and from ourselves. And in my perspective, we can apply the principle of interconnectedness most through recognizing that our actions are fed and sustained by a dependent relationship: focus, intent, goals and outcome.

Focus is knowing exactly what it is that we want and understanding what steps to take to achieve it; focus leads us to preparedness. Intent is the "why" and "how," the driving force that allows us to explore new arenas; intent propels us forward to realize our goals. Goals, of course, are the targets in our endeavors; but as we know, whether or not we reach our goals isn't a matter of desire, but action. Outcome, then, is the result of focus, intent and meeting our goals, as well as the impact (positive or negative) that it has on others; the quality of the outcome depends entirely on the previous elements. But really, could focus, intent, or even a goal have been met without a desired outcome in mind? All aspects of this relationship depend on the others. Think about it like returning a serve in tennis: If the tennis ball is the focus, then the perfect swing that drives the ball and places it in the opposite court is the intent; thus we meet our goal of returning the serve and realize the intended outcome through the strength of our efforts. One without the other leaves us incomplete.

Following this line of thinking will lead us to at least three Performance Challenges, which I will discuss. But first, let's agree to begin each day by asking at least these two questions: "What are my focus and my intent?" and "What key Performance Challenges will I encounter?"

Identifying Our First Performance Challenge

As we think about our focus and our intent, our first Performance Challenge is the Workplace – actually, it's *behavior* in the Workplace. The workplace is our greatest teacher. Here is where we are able to determine who we are, and what it is that we want. It is also the place where we treat people the way we feel about ourselves; where we are socially conditioned to learn to like things by watching others who like them; and where conflict is an occasion to practice respect and empathy.

If we remain aware, the workplace is where we encounter one of our most important risks. Why? Because it is here that we are confronted by our *own* behavior. It is here that we realize who we are capable of becoming, and how we respond when we are faced with a diversity of behaviors, and complex business challenges that we encounter every day. It is here that we learn about others as much as we learn about ourselves. The workplace provides us with the opportunity to excel, if we enjoy what we are doing, if our companies foster growth, and if we are able to develop and maintain productive relationships.

It is here that we learn how to operate as a part of a team. If you are an Assistant who is a star performer, you know that you don't operate in a vacuum; and you know that your success stems at least in part from your team relationships. This is the shining moment for successful Executive Assistants because you are adept at exercising political judgment and you are skilled in the art of conflict resolution. You are able to search for solutions that give each side the opportunity to compromise without losing face. You initiate and manage successful relationships with the Executives you support because you understand professional boundaries. Experience has taught Assistants to know the difference between report, rapport and real intimacy; and where each belongs. Thus, their tenor is professional, courteous and ethical.

Our Second Performance Challenge is Resistance to Change

Resistance to change undermines successful performance, both our own and others'. The burden of change rests with people at every level, and especially at the key administrative support levels. To survive in this diverse and global environment, Executive Assistants have the responsibility to play a central role in spearheading their offices through the changes in business strategy and the pains of the electronic office revolution.

Successful Executive Assistants know about reform and renewal, leadership, interdependence and how the ability to influence can have wide-reaching implications... even to world relations. Professional Assistants are efficient and effective, while they adapt to meet the changes and the inherent instability that we encounter in a dynamic, global business world.

Professional Assistants recognize that our exciting, competitive business environment, driven by change, creates unprecedented opportunities for those who choose to forge forward! They know that change is a positive experience that fosters solidarity, incorporates transition and progress. That change is the keystone for growth. Effective change means a permanent rekindling of individual creativity and individual responsibility.

Assistants know that in order to keep up with these dramatic changes, their advantage depends upon acquiring new knowledge and adopting an enthusiastic attitude toward learning new skills. Speed and ability are crucial; and Assistants' effectiveness truly will be measured by their capacity to learn and employ these new skills. No longer will their performance be measured by the implication of the Executive Assistant role, instead their influence will be determined by their ability to respond to change and by their individual contribution. Assistants' willingness to hone their skills, to strive to be the best and to meet organizational needs, will differentiate them as congenial and competitive workplace contributors.

Assistants are not expected to get stale. Why? Because if you are avid about something, you are always chasing knowledge in that area. It is important to note that some firms will hire from outside their companies, as they are unable to fill senior roles from within their ranks. CEOs tell us that when they search within, they find that individuals who project "old-fashioned" perspectives by clinging to the past and relying upon outdated techniques, have non-competitive skill levels, a lack of business acumen and inflexible attitudes that do not meet Executive expectations.

So, we are strongly encouraged to challenge ourselves to acquire current skills, to not be complacent and to keep on improving. The corollary for this reasoning is obvious: given these trends and outlooks, it is almost impossible to overstate the significance of the changing nature of the new work universe. It is dynamic, huge, complex, multifaceted and ever-changing. All the rules seem to be gone. Finding ways to remain flexible and resilient to adapt to these changes is the current and reliable imperative. Adjust your mindset. Rather than resist change, accept it and make it work to your benefit. Expand your responsibilities and demonstrate how much you can contribute to your company.

We have discussed how becoming comfortable on the "cutting edge" takes constant effort and attention, but also ensures constant growth and longevity. Remember that denying the cutting edge can land you on the cutting room floor. Resistance to change is antiquated thinking that will leave us with ordinary skills. This clearly is not a reliable strategy. What is essential is new learning, adaptability, creativity and innovative thinking.

Our Third Performance Challenge is Self-Sabotage

Mental preparation is the key to successful performance, no matter what the performance may be. All high achievers prepare themselves psychologically prior to their performance. This includes positive thinking, developing self-confidence, goal setting, motivation, and concentration. It is vital to have the proper attitude and the desire to win; it is equally important to know your limits.

So many of us get attached to rituals of failure where we sabotage our careers subconsciously. Here's one example of a disabling ritual: Procrastination! Ask yourself, are you a true "pro" in procrastination, so that the only choice remaining is to take immediate action? If you know this about yourself, then eliminating procrastination from your ritual will free you from ever allowing people to force you into a bad decision because of time constraints.

And there's more. There's Terry Orlick, Ph.D whose book, *In Pursuit of Excellence*, points to some self-limiting habits, as follows: "How much time do you spend in 'The Drama of Me?' Through studies, psychologists and neuroscientists have shown that people carry ongoing dialog, or self-talk, between 150 and 300 words a minute. This equates to between 45,000 and 51,000 thoughts a day. Self-talk reflects our belief in who we are. Beliefs, positive or negative, are literally etched into our brain in neural pathways. Unfortunately, most people relay more negative messages than positive messages through self-talk. Research has demonstrated that the words we tell ourselves about ourselves affect our performance, our self-esteem and our relationships. Learning how to recognize negative self-talk and change it into positive self-talk is an enormously necessary skill required for advancing one's level of performance. This may be done the same way it was created, through self-talk or affirmations. Anything that follows the phrase 'I am' is an affirmation, positive or negative."

We are profoundly influenced by what we say about ourselves. Think about this: With our words, we have the ability to help mold and shape the future of anyone with whom we experience relationship. This suggests that to change our language is to change our reality, and to switch our focus to being aware of others and what lies outside ourselves. You can't help someone else to be great if you don't feel great about yourself.

Carefully assessing our current rituals will enable us to determine whether they are empowering or self-limiting. Are we getting what we want from our current behaviors, patterns, and ideas? Albert Einstein also tells us that "once we accept our limits, we go beyond them." He also tells us that "imagination is more important than knowledge."

So, instead of self-limiting rituals, perhaps our effectiveness can instead be based on a commitment to established rituals of success. This means that we:

Focus on preparedness,

Make our *Intent* exploring new arenas,

Set *Goals* that are immediate, intermediate, long term.

Realize Outcome: The Result of Focus, Intent, Setting and Achieving Goals

With a commitment to these rituals of success, we are ready to meet head-on our workplace challenges. We are not haphazard. We do not let things "just happen" then react to them, because this allows situations to get away from us. We work with a deliberate plan. We accept that the responsibility for our actions resides with us, and not with those around us or our environment. We are able to empower ourselves to choose our responses to the stimuli of life. Our environment is to some extent determined by the choices we make. We take responsibility for the consequences of our decisions. Remember, we are more likely to excel and reach our goals if we enjoy what we are doing, if our companies foster growth and if we develop productive relationships.

We develop a passion for excellence, we make it a personal value. This changes us and affects the people around us. Excellence is achieved with a strong and forthright presentation of self, and it has a lasting influence.

Inside each of us is one of these brave, brilliant and daring characters. Yet, excessive fear and self-doubt can be the greatest detractors of personal genius. If fear is too strong, the genius is suppressed. It seems right to work toward a single objective: to take risks, to be bold, to let our genius convert that fear into power and brilliance.

To change thinking about change is to welcome it rather than to dread it. A reminder: Old ideas are our biggest liability simply because while that idea or way of doing something was an asset yesterday, yesterday is gone. You can do things the same way for years and look around one day and you're out of step. And that's neither good nor bad, it just is.

So, let me linger for a moment on the concept of meeting our goals: this forces us to think about what we are doing and why we are doing it, to scrutinize the norm, the well-accepted, standard approaches and policies and to look for a more appropriate, effective way of reaching our goals. If we are afraid of change and value our own security more than the great things that we might achieve, then we are not living a life of maximum impact on people, places and things in our world.

No matter where you live, or the business entity and Executives you support, you are responsible to create your own future! Learn to recognize opportunities as they open before you; learn to recognize the acknowledgements of your work well done. Avoid self-sabotage!

This reminds me of a CEO standing before a group giving a new directive: "We have streamlined the work week to become more effective. In doing so, we have reduced your work week to just one day, while keeping your pay at the same rate, and we have now designated Wednesday as the official workday...are there any questions?" A voice from the rear asks, "Does that mean we have to come in every Wednesday?"

EQ/IQ Case Story 5: **Leadership through Intrinsic Motivation, Self-Capital, and Self-Care**

Nose up, turbines roaring, air currents passing around its wings, the plane accelerates, free to climb higher. Naveen at the window watches the plane's diminishing shadow cast its translucence over motorways and rough terrain before yielding to a vast blue. "In 9 minutes and 35 seconds we'll be reaching our optimum cruising elevation, a steady 34,000 feet above sea level," the captain informs his passengers over the loudspeaker. Naveen, still fixed at the window, thinks about flying. *To experience this degree of mobility, this boundless height, I would never get bored of the journey. I'd live for the trip.*

The trip. Surrey was nice this time of year. Southwesterly winds carry the warmth inland from ocean currents, thawing the streets outside Autov8's expanded headquarters. Naveen visits England routinely to onboard new development teams; her knowledge of Scott's preferred creative concepts makes her an obvious choice for this assignment. Nearly one-hundred employees spend their first week with her, learning integrated design and functional aesthetics. Despite their enthusiasm, she has been on autopilot this trip.

For a long time, Naveen has supported Scott in their endeavor to bring utility to the user experience. Because of their partnership, she has risen in success with Scott, vertically climbing from Executive Assistant to Senior Executive Assistant, and now to Chief of Staff. That was the end goal, and she had made it.

Where was my enthusiasm? Naveen muses, thinking of Surrey. She enjoys traveling on Scott's behalf, welcoming global personnel into the fold. Getting to see their individual genius develop into one collective form is exciting. *I get to see that excitement; so why don't I feel it?* Sometimes success, when steady, causes stagnation, restlessness even. Her high degree of Emotional Intelligence confirms this and what needs to happen. *I've reached the top. Where else is there to go?* Indeed, the lifelong journey to Emotional Intelligence mastery requires finding new, challenging pathways to care for oneself emotionally, yes, but mentally and physically as well. *Have I been so focused on caring for others that I've overlooked caring for myself?*

In that moment, Naveen gets it: She's not at the ceiling of her perceived success. She's back on the ground floor, free to climb higher. *What is the ceiling other than a perception of how far one can go? The ladder can be lengthened...or widened. The mind can be reset.*

The plane is landing; she opens her eyes. She's home and it's evening here. The lights from the Motor City are coming alive. Turning on her phone, she taps the car service app and sends the driver a message before departing the plane. "Change of plans," it reads, "We won't be stopping by the office. I'd like to make it home in time for dinner."

The Takeaway. Modern life is suffused with converging emotions, brought on by the impact of age-related circumstances, and changing values. Some may find themselves wading through intra-personal conflict when these values are tested. The duality of this effect is that it can be one of the most overwhelming and revealing experiences in one's life, having multi-directional implications on not only those around us, but also throughout the workplace. The answer, of course, in terms of balancing the way forward, is applying the Emotional Intelligence toolkit.

The Toolkit. The turning point is a triangle of self-awareness and self-management that spotlights pivotal themes that we wish to change and repurpose, helping us reconnect to life and job satisfaction; two distinct entities with shared borders.

- Awaken

    o Self-reflection: Are you open to change? Do you have the willpower, or the tenacity, to change? Do you have the "waypower", as in, can you see a path clearly through the maze of your converging emotions, in order to change? Assess your current state versus your desired state. Ask yourself, where have you been? Where are you going? And what if…? Having a high-level of Emotional Intelligence makes you extraordinarily capable of welcoming change.

- Heal

    o Self-care: Develop an individual, self-investment plan that addresses your pursuit of achieving mental and physical wellbeing, using positive emotions (i.e., joy, gratitude, serenity, interest, hope, pride, amusement, inspiration, awe, and love) as your guide.

Whatever care event you choose, make sure it is something that you enjoy doing and not an energy-depleting chore. What small changes can you start making today?

- Evolve

  o Self-capital: We are successful when we are happy, and we are happy when we are challenged, and change is the catalyst for this sequence. In the pursuit of change, establish self-capital, or the intrinsic motivations and gains based on three values: human connection, passion, and meaning.

The Application. Devoting time to take care of oneself is the cornerstone of success. Self-care is bespoke. It is not selfish. Drawing on Emotional Intelligence will help us identify what our minds and bodies need to develop regular investment plans that will grow our emotional wealth. As a bonus, our newly minted self, supported by intrinsic motivators and gains, ensures competitive advantage because, unlike investments of infrastructure, self-capital is the one investment that cannot be duplicated.

CHAPTER XIII

Where Do We Go from Here?

Recent articles imply a vanishing or diminishing of the Executive Assisting Profession. This premise is based on a misperception and a lack of understanding of the purpose of the role. The arguments being offered target a particular demographic within the population of Assistants; namely, an older demographic who have not acquired a college degree, and who are perhaps lacking in real mastery of the latest technology. These circumstances do not imply a diminishing of the role; rather they speak to the challenges facing a particular demographic. This demographic is experiencing similar issues across virtually every sector and industry. These articles attempt to authenticate the role's implied limitations, and are substantiated by antiquated, underlying assumptions. It is now more vital than ever to challenge these hypotheses.

My 12 years as an Executive Assistant to a world leader, followed by 34 years of experience as President of a retained recruiting and consulting firm, operating on a global basis, specializing in the placement of Senior-Level Executive Assistants and Chiefs of Staff with business leaders worldwide, confirms that the Assisting career is not vanishing, This career is, in fact, expanding dramatically to meet the business goals and expectations of global Executives, who operate in a 24/7 business environment. The Executive Assistant role has expanded to such an extent that oftentimes one of our main tasks is to confirm an appropriate title to accommodate the new skills within these high-level positions. The broad spectrum of these contemporary descriptions confirms the change that is occurring to advance the vitality of this role. We are now in a landscape where position descriptions reflect titles that vary from Administrative Assistant to Executive Assistant to Senior-level Executive Assistant. Based on the diversity of our business practices, the title that informs this very senior role is that of Chief of Staff/Executive Life Manager.

Today, the tendency is that of a progressive leaning toward higher and higher levels of responsibility, where certain tasks can be shifted from the Executive to the Executive Assistant. The objective of the role is to save Executives' time, maximize their effectiveness, streamline processes, and repurpose procedures. This has become a more critical imperative since the 2008 economic downturn, when companies were forced to do more with less and Assistants across all industries began taking on functions that were traditionally delegated elsewhere, including project management, office management, and oftentimes an aspect of business management. Of course, this expanded portfolio necessitates new requirements that a traditional segment of the population may not have, thus posing challenges to that demographic within the role, as evidenced in recent articles.

The future of those whose talent opens the door to the Executive Assisting career is reflected in their ability to demonstrate the self-sustaining qualities, techniques and innovative skills that prepare them to welcome change now and in the future. Their intellectual vitality, their demonstrated management and leadership and strategic support skills give them the ability to create structure, systems, and procedures encouraged by technology solutions. These are the precise specifications that reinforce the imperative of this role while it greatly improves global workplace effectiveness.

Business leaders continue to face tremendous challenges, workforce issues, regulatory concerns, and globalization. Among decision-makers' greatest challenges is the effective and efficient management of their company's mission, their ability to lead change, and to offer growth opportunities for their existing staff. Demanding performance measures increase downward pressure on Executive teams. More than ever, decision-makers need trustworthy colleagues who translate directives, clarify their intent and purpose, help facilitate decisions, confirm objectives and achieve agreed-upon goals, including coordinating with others who might be involved. In this new and ceaselessly shifting world of work, disruption creates the need for the redefinition of Corporate Suite accountability. Adjustments are needed, and teams must align themselves around a new and ever-fluid work dynamic.

There is much for us yet to do but we need to start now by asking and acting, People don't know what they don't know – I'm sure you've heard that before. If we truly believe that our profession is misunderstood, then the first thing we need to do is inform and educate those in the business world to the reality of what we do. I believe we have reinforced that message throughout this book.

In addition, if we want to be valued for what we can bring to the table, we need to ask for a spot there. In so many cases, we fear rejection of our ask that we don't even try – why? The worst that could happen is that the answer is "no". And then we can ask "why" again. The "five whys" is one of the methods used in Green Belt training (Green Belt is an industry-recognized level of skill and knowledge that involves Six Sigma practices to gain optimal results within specific processes. The training addresses the root causes of these underlying issues to enable best practices to evolve – to get to the heart of the issue we are trying to solve).

I have found that when one provides appropriate reasoning around an "ask" and demonstrates the value it brings to all involved, the reasonable response will be a resounding "yes"! This has been my experience in several of the roles that I have held. I have "asked" for Executive Assistant presence at Leadership Meetings. I have "asked" for the same training for Executive Assistants within an organization that is usually reserved for only the top leadership of the company. Not only was I granted these asks, but the Executives and the companies have benefited greatly from them. Executive Assistants need to experience these learnings to be as effective as possible, for they are the ones to carry out the initiatives of their Executives.

When I talk about this at Executive Assistants' conferences, I am usually confronted with questions and concerns centered around the feeling that we, in this profession, just aren't important enough to our Executives for these "asks."

We need to value ourselves if we want others to value us. And we need to feel confident in our abilities. In one of my positions working for a CEO of a company, I was surprised and delighted to find that this particular CEO prepared me personally for the position at hand. He spent a week with me explaining the history of the company, his initiatives and his thinking, and the appropriate people that I should seek for different situations. After several months of working for this CEO, he told me that since he travelled 70-80% of the time, that when he was not available to make a decision, I must make it for him. That is why he wanted me to understand his thinking and reasoning behind his vision. I remember feeling hesitant because I was afraid of making a significant error and his answer was one that emboldened me for the rest of my career. He simply said, "As long as you don't kill anyone, we can fix it". It is so important to create a reciprocal relationship with the Executive you are supporting – to truly understand their thinking so that you can embrace or even challenge it; but you must understand it. That is why you have to have a seat at the table. And that is why you should not be afraid to ask for as much information as you believe you need to do your job as effectively as possible.

Co-author Loretta Sophocleous tells us that "not only should you educate yourself about the company, you should look for opportunities outside of the company as well." During her six-year tenure as President of C-Suite Executive Support Professionals (C-SESP) their yearly conferences for Executive Assistants differed from many conferences in that the subject matter was more focused on business rather than systems. Loretta and her team focused on subjects that our Executives would want to know – economics, AI, trends in business, cybersecurity, etc. I was amazed at the speakers we were able to secure – giants in their fields. And all it took was an "ask" from us. These were people with whom we came into contact during our daily business. They believed that what we were striving for was important, and because we had always treated them with respect and professionalism, they were more than happy to give of their time to speak to this group.

There is much for us yet to do but we need to start now by asking and acting. Remember Albert Einstein's reliable quote, "Imagination is more important than knowledge."

EQ/IQ Case Story 6: **The Emotionally Intelligent Support Leader**

"Is this everything?" Scott asks Naveen, while exiting the elevator. He was referencing the open report file on the tablet that she had just handed him. "Yes," Naveen answers. "That's everything you need, including the committee's four-point analysis for next steps. Everyone from CSR is ready in your conference room." Picking up the pace, the duo made their way to the Office of the CEO. "What's required, now, is my clear input and authority. You will pick up after I *'broaden and narrow'*" Scott tells her, opening the door. She knew what he meant: this meeting would require a fair amount of primer at the onset, such as highlighting the recent success of their CSR efforts to establish a trusting environment, broadening the committee's vision, and narrowing their focus for solving this looming problem.

"Hello, everyone," Scott greeted the room of Executives, choosing a seat at the front. As he began speaking, Naveen organized her thoughts, specifically on improving the performance of the committee, in the pursuit of a shared goal: extracting the right communication strategy. Naveen knew Scott wanted the committee to make the right decision for all stakeholders, particularly for their alliance with TechSmart, Autov8's largest retailer. TechSmart was in the news for reneging on a scheduled wage increase, and a coalition of their workforce had organized a regional walkout that was gaining in popularity online. The issue for Autov8 was that this dispute overshadowed their annual product update and ran counter to the corporate social responsibility (CSR) program that Autov8 had launched in tandem with the product, a product that received premium shelf placement at all of TechSmart's locations. Being on the wrong side of this issue would cost them.

Scott had finished, and it was Naveen's turn. "I have asked Naveen to bring us current on our TechSmart response options," announced Scott. She was focused and prepared, emotionally balanced. Years of practicing how to be mindful, to coexist with positive and negative emotions, gave way to consciousness, optimism, and leadership. She was an emotionally intelligent Chief of Staff leading *with* others.

"I trust we've all had time to review the report," said Naveen. "I'd like Allie to lead us through the agenda items, and then everyone will have the opportunity to discuss their department's recommendations." Naveen had a talent for developing others, creating opportunities for additional voices to try their hand at bolstering their achievement orientation.

Naveen looked over to Scott as the report's findings

were reviewed aloud by the committee's members. His nonverbal cues suggested he was pleased with the report's completeness. The week prior, Naveen had e-mailed each member a request to prepare a decentralized strategy within their respective business units, and then Allie assembled the information into one report for advanced review. Her initiative worked; shifting the committee's focus from information-sharing to decision-making made the best use of limited time.

When the meeting opened to discussion and debate, Naveen relied on her cultural awareness to decode the context-specific dialogue exchanged between the committee's members, several of whom were multinational as well as multidisciplinary. Mark, the Executive Director of Finance, tended to engage pragmatically. This was evidenced when he spoke: "We need to be smart with this," he said, "and, forgive me for saying, I don't see how these recommendations are necessarily smart for us. I think we need to speak to the operational costs involved and draft a formal performance contract before we decide on messaging."

"That's a valid point, Mark." Naveen knew to adjust her leadership dial based on situational need and audience. "I agree with you. We need to specify the resources required to execute. Let's schedule a final sign-off meeting once the contract details are specified." Naveen knew she needed to redirect Mark's focus while Scott is here; Scott is more creative and less analytical. "I suggest we stay on message strategy and how our sustainability framework can be embedded in the value-chain so as not to upset our customer base or our relationship with TechSmart." In working with Mark, Naveen's social awareness picked up on him valuing straightforwardness and transparency.

Two hours later, the CSR committee formed a solid service-oriented messaging strategy with a dual focus on building back consumer-retailer confidence. The meeting adjourned and the committee dispersed.

Naveen hung back to collect her things. Two knocks on the table, and she lifted her head. It was Scott. "Thanks for taking care of that, Navi," he said with gratitude. *Thanks,* she thought. It was another and always appreciated event.

The Takeaway. As someone who has spent her career simplifying the Executive landscape, Naveen's wide-ranging capacity to care for others speaks to her ability to lead with others. Here, Naveen confronted a problem and guided the Executive's Committee until a decision was reached, using a combination of personal and social communication competencies. She reality-tested a stressful situation, opening the conversation to a diverse decision-making body with unique perspectives grounded in the values of social responsibility and care equity, ensuring utility was met and shared among all stakeholders. Finally, Naveen kept to her vision of who she wanted to be – an emotionally intelligent support leader. She is an expert communicator and partnership builder. Her organizational awareness is supported by her active interest in attaining the best possible outcome for the good of the enterprise. She is a facilitator of individual progress, and a coach for when teams experience impediments of all kinds. Most importantly, she is the one entrusted to create the ecosystem for which the Executive can thrive.

The Toolkit. Not all problems (opportunities) are created equal, but we manage them using a common "broad vision to narrow focus" practice. To help you develop your own problem-solving process, the broad-to-narrow approach to decision making is a useful framework centered on building emotional awareness and acting on emotional information, aiding you, the support leader, in taking decisive action when presented with opportunities for growth and change.

- **Decode** emotional information.

Consider the context, or the emotional climate in which the transfer of meaning from one person to another takes place.

- There are personal, social, and environmental distinctions in how emotions are transferred. The EI support leader can sense and make sense of this emotional information, seeing things as they truly are.

- Improve the quality of the context and your communications by exhibiting a combination of support leader characteristics, outward manifestations of inward capabilities, like preparedness, knowledgeability, professionalism, altruism, sportsmanship, conscientiousness, optimism, empathy, and fellowship, just to name a few. Evaluate positive and negative emotions objectively, setting the stage to solve problems optimally and communicate well with others, getting the job done.

- Positivity begets positivity, and yet, there is value in experiencing uncomfortable, negative emotions sometimes, at the right time, thereby encouraging serendipitous outcomes. Of the six essential emotions – anger, disgust, fear, happiness, sadness, surprise – the EI support leader knows how to make negative emotions work for them and in ways that lead to higher-level mental functioning, emotional awareness, and emotional regulation.

- **Develop** emotional information.

  Use the broad-to-narrow approach to manage emotions and improve divergent thinking.

- State the real cause of the problem – not the related symptom – seeing the big picture and the finer details.

- Orient yourself with the problem, gathering facts, analyzing data, filtering useful information and bias, and defining unknowns and realistic worst-case scenarios.

- List and prioritize solutions that will accommodate the ever-changing circumstances. Draft solution ideas (critical thinking, creative brainstorming, and/or visual representations like decision trees) adherent to the situation, the problem solvers' skills and ethical values, and the future needs of the organization.

- **Direct** emotional information

  Use the broad-to-narrow approach to manage emotions and improve convergent action.

- Validate the best solution(s) based on criteria that is ranked for success, being open to problem solvers' emotions and viewpoints, and tailoring your communication strategy to one that resonates with them, in effect energizing their emotions. In moments of ambiguity, adding more voices to the discussion, from varying levels of management, encourages smarter, more diverse alternatives and promotes rapid decision making and execution.

- Enact the solution(s), engaging problem solvers and the organization's role responsibilities. To mitigate risk, juxtapose action-based questions throughout the solution process ("Is there a better way to accomplish this goal?"); this will stimulate the problem solvers' emotional intellects and mental acuities, leading to more effective and efficient "solutionizing."

- Review and evaluate the change outcome for continuous learning and improvement. If there is no change, return to an earlier development stage and rethink the process. Broad-to-narrow is a dynamic and subjective problem-solution approach that is unique to the problem solvers' emotionality as it is uniquely applied to the problem/opportunity.

The Application. Communication is the currency of leadership. We become better support leaders when we understand how the transfer of emotional information impacts problem solving, opportunity discovery, and decision making. The emotionally intelligent support leader leads not with positional power but with communication immersed in active learning and the promise of joint contribution, inclusivity, and fulfilling work.

EQ / IQ

CHAPTER XIV

Executive Life Manager: The Emerging Power Partnership

Part I. Repurposing the role of the Professional Executive Assistant.

The Executive Assistant profession is now an even greater career option than ever before. The core function and purpose of the Executive Assistant is one that has yet to be and, in my opinion, will not be replaced by the advances in modern technology or artificial intelligence. The competence and ingenuity applied in the execution of this position are certainly evolving, not to the detriment of the function itself, but rather to facilitate the higher level of responsibility the role now engenders.

I underscore the ever-increasing importance of the critical role of the Executive Assistant, as the context and content of the position shifts to meet current workplace demands and the role becomes more strategic in nature. My experience confirms that the skills of management, leadership and global business are now essential. Accordingly, the formula we have created that best represents the current and future role's performance strategy is: Leadership + Management + Strategic Support

= Business Partnership. The Executive/Executive Assistant Business Partnership reflects a unique work model, that requires the ability to adapt to and apply new skills, with the aptitudes and attitudes that enable individuals and companies to operate at high administrative levels.

Further advancement in this role is acknowledged by the title Chief of Staff/Executive Life Manager. This pathway to Chief of Staff/Executive Life Manager begins with an agile workforce that meets the challenges of the 21st Century. These transitions reflect this population's intelligent mind, professional practices, and strong determination to learn, respond to change, apply, and succeed.

In an economy that demands that we do more with less, global corporate leaders are relying more on their Executive Assistants and are positioning them as indispensable members of their senior leadership teams. Executive Assistants clearly have transitioned into a new normal with demanding specialized skills, relevant experience, increased personal aptitude and a commitment to exacting professional standards. Armed with these talents, career Executive Assistants face a rewarding and fulfilling future.

The traditional way of managing the Executive Assistant role has been transformed by new learning about how things can be done with speed and efficiency. The overarching principles and professional aspects that represent this role require that Executive Assistants fill the capability gap in conceptual, operational effectiveness and solution-based intuitive new ways of thinking. I cannot stress enough how willingness to change is this population's key strength; how innovative thinking becomes the new commodity.

There is nothing static about this role. A current and future perspective and performance standard has emerged. What is of primary importance is the ability to bring global and business knowledge and advanced technology applications to meet the essential requirements of this evolved role. A new job description has also emerged: In addition to the "classic" functions of Executive support, today's Executive Assistants must embody leadership and have the mind of an Executive-level manager, they must be analytical and administrative in their efforts, and have the skills and composure necessary to find and provide simple solutions to complex problems. Their acquired experience in human interaction to manage expectations in our world, which is comprised of cultural, demographic, and multicultural diversity, creates the right conditions and circumstances for Executives to achieve success.

Offered here is a valuable conversation about the workplace and the purpose of the 21st Century Executive Assistant, while considering six key questions:

- What does the recent trajectory of business suggest about the future of the Executive Assistant role?
- What constitutes relationship management at the Executive Assistant level?
- What defines an effective partnership with the Executive?
- What are the impossible demands placed on the Executive Assistant?
- What is required to change the perception of the Executive Assistant from being a cash-center to a value-delivery center?

–   How do Executive Assistants continue to maintain a competitive advantage?

Question #1: *What does the recent trajectory of business suggest about the future of the Executive Assistant role?*

With the rapid, almost exponential growth of technology and globalized markets in recent years, business and how it is conducted have taken on a markedly different appearance. This could lead many to believe that the Executive Assistant, the "informational attaché" of corporate Executives, is fading from relevance. Indeed, what purpose could it serve to employ a person when all that they do can be replicated by pushing a few buttons on a pocket-sized device?

It need not be explained how narrow and misinformed this idea is, but for emphasis, let's say it anyway: anyone who thinks this way could not be more wrong. The recent trajectory of business, if anything, indicates an even greater need for the presence of individuals who have always been more than any machine ever could be. Executive Assistants bring intimate knowledge of corporations and Executive mindsets, along with education and dynamic skills that go beyond simply accomplishing tasks, and ideas that go beyond improving tasks. Executive Assistants bring an interest and attention that can only come from personal investment. They bring a care and commitment that grows with the strength of their business partner relationship. And the more that the business world (and the world as a whole) changes, the more commitment and attention it will need. As Executives continue to brave the changing business landscape, they will continue to need another set of eyes, another sharp mind, and most importantly, another beating heart to face and manage the challenges ahead.

Question #2: *What constitutes relationship management at the Executive Assistant level?*

At any level, relationship management depends on communication and reliability. Executive Assistants' considerable degree of professionalism primes them to meet these criteria, and it is the quality of their character that allows them to exceed them. The individuals in this critical position of support understand that diligence in their communication (reaching out, responding in a timely and consistent fashion, ensuring their correspondence is received, etc.) establishes their commitment to the success of their relationships, while an even temper and egalitarian disposition invite others to respond in kind. A measured balance of humility and confidence make Executive Assistants approachable, and flexibility (both social and mental) makes them sought after by colleagues. Professional Executive Assistants' workplace contribution is shaped predominantly by the principles and best practices that advance new knowledge and professionalism in the role in order to surpass expected standards. Lastly, competence and dedication to "make good" on their word and expectations solidifies Executive

Assistants' reliability and makes a continued relationship with them both the "right" choice and the "desired" choice.

Question #3: *What defines an effective partnership with the Executive?*

Skills are an essential part of any working partnership, but to examine what makes a partnership *effective*, we must look beyond skills and into the *relationship* of the individuals involved. If mutual trust and respect are the building blocks of an effective partnership, open and clear communication is its cornerstone. This type of communication is a two-way street where Executive and Executive Assistant can suggest and agree upon ideas and expectations and align their goals in the interest of success. It is a business/personal arena where the understanding is that success is shared, both in its achievement and in its enjoyment. And it demands from one end a selfless level of support, a willingness to go the extra mile to see things done and done well... just as much as it deserves a humble and open appreciation and acknowledgment from the other.

This brings our focus to the other critical element of the effective partnership: compatibility. We have previously referred to the "personality fit factor" as a key component in the Executive/Executive Assistant partnership, and with good reason. The level of communication and synchronization described above cannot be fabricated or forced; person-to-person compatibility is the unseen constant, the "secret ingredient" that permeates all aspects of a partnership's success. When personalities "fit", they can complement each other's strengths and supplement each other's deficits. Furthermore, they can anticipate and rely on one another without hesitation. Mutual trust and respect, the building blocks; communication, the cornerstone; and compatibility, the cement that holds it all in place. And there is even more beyond the "perfect fit"; there is agreement in vision, there is agreement in the work at hand, there is a shared view of excellence and effectiveness, all of which are found within a Thought Partnership.

Question #4: *What are the impossible demands placed on the Executive Assistant?*

To start, "impossible" is a perception. Often times, as it is in this case, things appear "impossible" because external constraints and limitations create a sense of powerlessness that cannot be overcome. But if we could perhaps shift our perspectives even a few degrees, we might find that "impossible" is in fact within reach. So, what are these demands?

Executive Assistants are expected to have an all-encompassing skillset, be it clerical, technical, technological, or managerial, with no exception, no matter how things change over time. They must maintain absolute availability and possess a pre-emptive level of thinking and understanding (see: read minds). It is expected that Assistants be clear in all communication, regardless of the clarity (or lack thereof) of others. Likewise, they are to field all ranges of personalities and emotions with a consistent, almost elevated, calm. Most "impossible" of all, Executive Assistants must restructure time itself to meet all demands and deadlines in a timely fashion, without fail.

All humor aside, these expectations could seem impossible without the proper perspective. Consider for now that Executive Assistants, or rather, the individuals who pursue this career, are the type of people who take on challenges as a passion, and who work to transform complexity into something simple and manageable; something "possible". With that in mind, how Executive Assistants can achieve the impossible will be uncovered in the following two questions.

Question #5: *What is required to change the perception of the Executive Assistant from being an overhead cost to a value-delivery center?*

As discussed, there has been a historic ambiguity to naming the Executive Assistant Profession in order to appropriately define and reflect its responsibilities. Defining the position properly is a good starting point for perception change, one that entails a wide-scale incentive of understanding how pivotal Executive Assistants are to corporate success.

Acknowledging the high-level contributions Executive Assistants make internally and externally for a company demands acknowledging their capability and efficacy as leaders and managers. Recognizing the degree of education required to function in the Executive Assistant position, along with the need for continued education, validates their individual intelligence and creates space to support their growth. Taking into account Assistants' broad range of skills, along with the adaptability shown when applying said skills, identifies their indispensability and the unique impact they have on a daily basis. Appreciating the extent of patience, tact, and flexibility necessary to facilitate true support places distinct worth on the intrinsic qualities that often go unnoticed. Finally, when taking all aspects into consideration, providing appropriate and competitive compensation is the logical next step in acknowledging, appreciating, and respecting the value Executive Assistants bring to their Executives and the companies for which they work.

Question #6: *How do Executive Assistants continue to maintain a competitive advantage?*

We know that in a rapidly growing, ever-changing business climate, Executive Assistants must stay current and stay educated. They must be courageous in expanding their role by taking on new responsibilities and have the confidence to meet the expectations set along the way. Assistants must master the craft of time management by anticipating trends, personalities, and outcomes and adapting on the fly. They must go beyond willingness to accommodate change; they must expect change and prepare for it. This means educating, constantly, and applying what was learned with conviction, secure that the contribution is valid and valuable.

And it must be stated that this depends as much on the Executive Assistants as it does on the companies they support; the employer who invests in the "competitive advantage" of the Executive Assistant can provide the opportunities for education, provide the recognition that justifies that growing confidence, provide the perspective change that places the Executive Assistant in a position of value. In this position, external constraints and limitations disappear. In this position, anything is possible.

The Emergence of the New Profession

What skills and attitudes do the global workforce need to cultivate? What makes someone indispensable in today's global economy? The answers to these questions confirm an intellectual endeavor that demands vitality and enthusiasm. Passion + Purpose + Strategy + Focus = Impact. Executive Assistants will demonstrate creativity in every area of the talent and skill that they have acquired to pursue extraordinary achievement.

The pathway to the right skills and attitude can be found in one's ability to Reenergize, Redefine, Rediscover, Repurpose:

Reenergize... through intellectual innovation. Be smart in ways the Executive is not.

Redefine... your role. A new level of performance responsibility has emerged.

Rediscover... the road to success. Willingness to change is a key strength.

Repurpose... through relentless learning. Ongoing education is your best survival tactic.

The need is evident for qualified Professional Executive Assistants with specific management and decision-making skills, through which superb results and intellectual leadership is achieved. In this shifting world of work, business leaders who are most effective at optimizing talent will recognize and offer growth opportunities and economic rewards to those who are eager to advance, and who have an unflinching commitment to quality, the attitude to work collaboratively, the stamina to assist business leaders in meeting their business objectives, and a willingness to adapt to change. An internal "people movement strategy" can be an effective tool in advancing much of today's workforce who regard transience as a matter of course.

With so much variation and volatility, human capital management has become increasingly complicated. The term "war for talent" is no accidental representation; finding, developing and retaining top performers has become one of the greatest workplace challenges. Leaders must address and play a central role in this reality; it is an essential component of a company's strategy. Understanding this reality gives access to the means of becoming an indispensable contributor to a company's success.

Professional Executive Assistants who rise to the C-Suite are known for their silent power. They now are perfectly positioned to assume this expanded role. They are reliable in this transition because of their adaptability to change, motivation, insight and determination, which thereby transform business culture.

This newly-devised, hybrid role, from Executive Assistant to Chief of Staff/ Executive Life Manager, is an inevitable new category that combines traditional support and strategic management, and with the right performance standards, will fill the unaddressed gap that now exists between operations, support and overall management of the Executive office. The new value of this role is its impact on Executive productivity. With absolute trust, confidentiality, objectivity, clarity, judgment and the confidence of the Executive, this individual is the main liaison, thinks like the Executive, sees the business as a whole, knows and understands the Executive's intent, observes him/her in action, distinguishes nonverbal reactions and responds accordingly. This trusted colleague provides the efficiency and structure with the ability to manage the mundane and the profound, respond to the shifting needs of the workplace, optimize the use of technological platforms, represent the Executive internally and externally, solve day-to-day problems, provide the interface to ensure things get done, and manage differences through collaboration.

The Differentiator: The Traditional Role of Chief of Staff

While largely prominent in government, the acknowledged talent of the Chief of Staff has gained momentum in the private sector and is increasingly perceived as a critical role in the leadership team.

The traditional Chief of Staff role is an integral part of an internal professional and leadership development strategy that addresses some of the challenges in the business world today and can provide companies with a competitive advantage. The Chief of Staff role facilitates the CEO's vision while enabling other members of the leadership team to work together effectively to identify and achieve company goals. This role is acknowledged as a means to extend the reach of C-Suite Executives, to fill organizational gaps and complement missing skillsets, to provide a professional path, a development tool and horizontal expansion for those who facilitate the CEO's priorities. The content of this role can vary based on the person in the role and for whom they work; thus, it can be difficult to hire from the outside versus providing expansion opportunities for existing, talented employees.

An overview of the role of the traditional Chief of Staff describes this individual as someone who generally works behind the scenes to solve CEO/organizational problems, spearheads new projects, and maximizes the CEO's time and focus. This individual works directly with CEO's direct reports, resolving conflicts and issues as they arise. Often, they act as confidante and advisor to the Chief Executive, serving as a sounding board for ideas. The private sector role especially requires the proactive identification of issues that could impact the successful execution of the CEO's commitments and responsibilities, which include conducting Board meetings and a heavy reliance on frequent travel. The Chief of Staff makes the CEO aware of and brings his/her focus and attention to challenging issues, providing a framework and positioning of innovative ideas, to help resolve recurring problems and mitigate risk. This is a foundational shift that requires that CEOs and C-suite Executive Assistants define efficient ways to succeed together.

The Indispensable Role for C-Suite Executive Assistants: Chief of Staff/Executive Life Manager

The benefits of this internal development model embody two levels of expertise:

- Level 1: Essential experience and ongoing learning for improvement

- Level 2: The indispensable opportunity to transform the essential role and to capitalize on innovation.

Both are critical aspects that deserve in-depth analysis.

Level 1: *Essential experience and ongoing learning for improvement*

In contrast to the traditional Chief of Staff position, the Executive Assistant who has acquired the role of Chief of Staff/Executive Life Manager differs in that this individuals offers experience in CEO interface and support, ensures the integrity and delivery of the administrative support mandate, is business savvy, mission driven, and serves as a human database, with the confidence, knowledge and capability to structure an efficient operating framework to successfully implement the CEO's directives. This individual has the added value of insight and in-depth reality of the needs, perspectives, expectations, goals and personality of the CEO; thus, decisions made on the CEO's behalf are sustained by this competitive advantage.

Level 2: *The indispensable opportunity to transform the essential role and to capitalize on innovation .*

Extending the Executive's reach, as described above, will be expedited if the Chief of Staff/Executive Life Manager has already been successful within the organization, especially as the Senior Executive Assistant. This individual knows how to get things done, has effective relationships with internal and external stakeholders, understands the company, is a cultural fit, and has a proven track record of effectiveness in translating the Executive's vision into action. Filling this role from the outside greatly decreases the new Chief of Staff/Executive Life Manager's opportunities for success. Why? This trusted colleague has an acute understanding of the personalities, expectations, standards, and competing imperatives that drive decisions.

The Chief of Staff/Executive Life Manager becomes the key member within the Executive Suite brain trust who is tasked with transforming the challenge of change to the rewards of increased productivity and profitability. How? Through innovation. The Chief of Staff/Executive Life Manager knows that innovation is a new method or idea that improves efficiency. Peter Drucker tells us that "Innovation is change that creates a new dimension of performance." Technological innovation has ushered in a disruptive change in how business is developed and maintained. We are in a technological world and access to innovation has become, by far, its most beneficial byproduct. Innovation, however, as all else, must be managed.

There is a clear parallel between the principles that represent indispensability and innovation because one begets the other. Innovation, like indispensability, can be achieved methodically: understand where opportunities lie and have a strategic plan; a road map to achieve goals and priorities to make a difference, not just to complete a task. Indispensability is confirmed by integrity, selflessness, diplomatic resilience, and emotional stability. Innovation and indispensability, hallmark measures of the effective Executive Assistant, create the transferable value for the platform for the role of the Chief of Staff/Executive Life Manager, and its resultant impact on amplified Executive productivity.

Part II. The Executive Assistant Path to Chief of Staff/ Executive Life Manager

How does the Executive Assistant achieve the level of Chief of Staff/Executive Life Manager? Embrace the change or stay behind.

In my work with CEOs, I have learned that within the 21st century business environment, an ideal hire would be a Chief of Staff/Executive Life Manager. The quality of strategic decisions and the ability to deliver successful outcomes, while saving Executives' time, are what make this unique role essential and indispensable.

A trusted advisor, the Chief of Staff/Executive Life Manager, facilitates the CEO's vision while enabling other members of the leadership team to work together effectively to identify and achieve company goals. A critical member of the leadership team, the Chief of Staff is responsible for overall administrative management of the Executive's office, internal and external communications, and coordination of company-wide efforts. This is a uniquely qualified individual who possesses the focus, flexibility, and strategic skills necessary to facilitate decisions on behalf of the Executive. It is a singularly explicit skill set that evolves from ever-mounting business pressures placed on the Executive Suite resulting from the advent of technology-driven business and the accelerated globalization of commerce.

Executive Assistants must adapt a learning strategy that links traditional knowledge with the new knowledge and skills necessary to meet the challenge of this enhanced role. Managing logistics, leading projects and strategic initiatives require Executive/Executive Assistant collaborative solutions.

The best predictor of future behavior, so the saying goes, is past behavior. What better way to increase the odds that the newly appointed Chief of Staff/Executive Life Manager will be successful in the role (and minimize the disruption) than by filling this role with the individual who has already proven that he/she knows how to get things done within the organization; the individual who has built relationships with key stakeholders, understands the company's mission and culture, and has a proven track record of effectively translating the Executive's intent into action?

It makes sense: the more complex the landscape (the higher the stakes, and the greater the need to make critical decisions with limited information), the more a leader must have someone by his or her side who is committed to advancing the leader's agenda. If, as the "Commander-in-Chief," you need to rely on someone in "the heat of battle," you must be able to trust that the person responsible for the flow of information and the management of your time has no competing interests. The challenge and opportunity for the Executive is to reimagine the Executive Assistant role and, in doing so, create a re-fortified firewall around the Executive's mission, management and leadership team.

The Chief of Staff/Executive Life Manager position requires the proactive identification of issues that could impact the successful execution of the Executive's commitments. These are issues about which the Executive should be made aware while framing/positioning ideas to resolve the problem and mitigate the risk. These responsibilities are represented in the chart below:

The Chief of Staff/Executive Life Manager effectively manages internal and external communications with the ability to be an extension of the Executive and his/her face to the public. This transformed role demands the ability to think about what the Executive needs to do to accomplish his/her goals, and to organize accordingly.

The Chief of Staff/Executive Life Manager establishes the operating framework to successfully implement the Executive's directives. An imperative is to design the Executive's time to support purpose and clear outcomes.

Part III. Creating the Parallel Track: The Evolution of the hybrid role of Executive Assistant to Chief of Staff/ Executive Life Manager

Our success will depend as much on constant innovation as on cost efficiency. Given these trends and outlooks, the opportunity to capitalize on innovation, to realize advanced technological accomplishment, and to streamline administrative strategic support are the important components of the Chief of Staff/Executive Life Manager position that facilitate the Executive's vision. This is intellectual progress. The Executive Assistant who has achieved this level of performance should be encouraged and recognized, should experience an appropriate reward system, and should be offered training on an on-going basis.

For the Executive Assistant, it is to accept the challenge and opportunity of this new hybrid role as both strategic support and management, and to be recognized for that contribution. Ever-evolving demands require that Executive Assistants seamlessly alternate between assisting, accommodating, and asserting, and sometimes to perform in all three capacities at once. This continuous blending of support, management, and leadership translates to a new level of business partnership between the Executive and the Executive Assistant.

The effective Executive and Chief of Staff/Executive Life Manager team can immediately respond to the high-velocity change in the work environment, to the hyper-speed of technology, and to competitive world events that affect business strategies. Executive success now is dependent upon this new talent. The Chief of Staff/ Executive Life Manager's mission is to be relied on to make the Executive's vision a reality. The purpose is to meet the goals of the Executive and the enterprise, with a focus on consistency, creativity, and global communication. We have been incorporating these skills into this transformed role in incremental steps.

The complexity and rate of change that global businesses confront today provide some clues as to why the Chief of Staff/Executive Life Manager position can be seen in companies of almost every size and structure, and within every market sector. The expansion within the role is realized by the career Assistant's ability to take on more and more functions on behalf of the Executive, allowing the Executive to focus on business-sustaining practices. The Executive and the organization have the challenge and opportunity to create this new hybrid position to fill a critical need, and the Professional Executive Assistant has the challenge and opportunity to hone his/her skills and knowledge to take on this enhanced role.

Unquestionably, technology performs some aspects of the work Assistants used to do. Accordingly, Assistants must advance their skills with new learning, so that they leverage this technology and use the data/computing power/intelligent assistance now available to add value. The imperative is to determine efficiencies in order to save time and contribute to revenue, to make recommendations, elevate the experience of the Executive by assimilating rapidly what is available to you and applying that to what YOU know to be important (goals/priorities/expectations of the Executive).

Technology can be overwhelming; however, Professional Assistants are not paralyzed by the challenge because they master it and enjoy the learning energy they have not experienced before, when they simply were being allowed to execute tasks. Now, they take things to a higher level and, with their insight, wisdom, discernment, and empathy/sensitivity, they deliver value beyond basic, even flawless, execution.

Technology is our greatest ally and asset. Today's Assistant embraces it, while remaining obsessively curious about it. They read voraciously (especially in areas new to them), savor every nugget of learning and let it whet their appetite for more and more knowledge/know-how. They have fun in making the application of technology a resolvable challenge, a skill for which they are recognized.

A few takeaways regarding technology:

- Technology is applied to Chief of Staff/Executive Life Manager's strategy for personal and professional success.

- Understand the drivers of economic growth and competitive advantage in order to leverage technology to reach goals.

- Intellectual growth is free; the information and tools for new learning and expansion within the role are readily available in the modern day.

Assistants understand goals and strategy and use judgment based on experience. This means that Professional Executive Assistants must work harder with diligence and resiliency as their expansion tool. They must reinvent themselves; recognize opportunity accept that intellectual consistency is required, and that new learning is an imperative. What is now required is:

A keen understanding of economic trends and global events.

The importance of government regulations on business.

General business and industry knowledge.

General business savvy: digital innovation.

This marks an important new stage of challenge and opportunity in the evolution and professionalization of the role of the Executive Assistant. And their choices affect the workplaces we all inhabit.

Business leaders' attention is focused on designing, motivating, leading and building the administrative management team, which includes Executive-Suite Support, by acknowledging those who can serve as advocate and strategist, influence policies and corporate decisions, and develop others. The Executive and Executive Assistant team is now at the center of this work environment, where technological advancements and competitive world events are affecting business strategies.

These increasing dictates demand that the traditional way of managing the Executive Assisting role be revolutionized by learning how more complex tasks and projects can be done better and faster, all within the context of a strategic understanding of the Executive's goals. This is the serious business of the Executive Assistant of which successful execution requires performance far beyond "the same, but more". This is a fundamental shift that requires that Executives and Executive Assistants must devise efficient ways to work together. This is the opportunity to fill a widening gap in support of the Executive, and the organization, while offering the experienced Executive Assistant the opportunity to accept the challenge of this hybrid support/management role that combines operational efficiency and strategic agility.

The three pillars of the Chief of Staff/Executive Life Manager platform are represented as Digitally Sophisticated, Intellectually Reliable, and Global Business Savvy. Great leaders excel at recognizing and developing talent. Talented Executive Assistants are specialized professionals, who know that new learning is an absolute imperative to improve efficiency. The takeaway is that a well-supported Executive is an effective Executive.

Imagine Corporate Responsibility:

Imagine position descriptions that describe and outline skills that are appropriate for Executive Life Managers. Imagine that companies will now put into place compensation systems that align with Executive Life Managers' contribution and commitment. Imagine that companies will invest in their education with the same emphasis as is offered to executives. Imagine that companies will hire the right people for the position and assure position clarity. This role must be given great prominence, with new position descriptions, new titles and commensurate compensation.

The best thing in our lives is the gift of imagination and free will. Imagine what you would like to be and create it. The formula followed by all geniuses is to do what you like to do best and do it to the very best of your ability. So, do what you love; and train to be your best.

The times ahead promise to be banner years for those who embrace a Business Partnership with the Executives they support. Be ready and stay alert for the opportunities that will arise within our ever-changing business landscape. Assistants: continue to prepare your career for leadership from the greatness of which you are made.

What is the Future of Executive Assisting?

The future is you. In completing this book, you are ahead of the game. You represent the opportunity of learning, the commitment to your profession, and the model for global support leadership, where partnership and indispensability intersect at its core. Together, our assisting community represents a new frontier for being, a movement not defined by industry, geography, or person, but by our collective capabilities and passions. This movement, in essence, is a formula – a world-class assistant's formula – made to represent your Emotional Intelligence, Cultural Intelligence, and Systems Intelligence: (EI + CI + SI) = (Success + Satisfaction).

Emotional Intelligence, in practice, is every smart decision we have made. Because it is a keystone ability, its all-encompassing domains support **Cultural Intelligence**, which increases our means to connect and work inter-culturally, regionally, organizationally, generationally, and ideologically. **Systems Intelligence,** the whole being greater than the sum of its individual parts, represents doing things right and doing things better within our systemic contexts and everyday lives. Combining Emotional Intelligence (EI), Cultural Intelligence (CI), and Systems Intelligence (SI) is the dynamic formula that represents a new frontier in executive assisting that allows us to thrive in tomorrow's global marketplace.

Colleague to colleague, I supportively challenge you to use this formula along with the purposeful stories and discussions within this book. I encourage you to create a personal self-development plan – unique to you, and for you – aimed at finding your success and satisfaction that secures your place at the leadership table, ensuring that your rise is not by luck or happenstance but by merit and design.

It takes real effort to adopt a challenge like this, but if

is one thing that we know about each other, it is that your best efforts as Professional Executive Assistants are – bar none – above the rest.

You are the future of work.

EQIQ Mastery Class with Melba Duncan

Join Melba and Her Team in an online, 12-Segment Mastery Class on Enhanced Emotional Intelligence and Career Advancement.

Master *EQ/IQ* with Melba and the *EQ/IQ* team. Enrich Career Management, Social Awareness, and Relationship Management skills through chapter key point and Case Story discussion and mastery.

You will learn:

How to reframe priorities; manage 'into', rather than 'from'; how to effectively articulate your career vision; how to increase your personal and corporate value.

- Compact, 30-minute professional development segments
- Join major influencers in your career path
- Exclusive, ongoing post-seminar training and support

WATCH AN INTRODUCTORY VIDEO: EAEQIQ.COM

Readings and Resources

There are many, many good resources that can help you intentionally increase your Emotional Intelligence.

Arbinger Institute. *Leadership and Self Deception: Getting Out of the Box.* Oakland, CA: Berrett-Koehler Publishers, October 2009.

Drucker, Peter F. *The Essential Drucker.* New York, NY: HarperCollins, October 2009.

Goleman, Daniel. *Emotional Intelligence: Why It Can Matter More Than IQ.* New York, NY: Bantam, September 2005.

Kurzweil, Ray. *The Singularity is Near: When Humans Transcend Biology.* New York, NY: Penguin, January 2007

Orlick, Terry. *In Pursuit of Excellence.* Champaign, IL: Human Kinetics, Inc., November 2015

Tharp, Twyla. *The Creative Habit: Learn It and Use It for Life.* New York, NY: Simon&Schuster, October, 2003

Wiersma, Bill. *The Power of Professionalism: The Seven Mind-Sets That Drive Performance and Build Trust.* Ravel Media, January 2011

Wiersma, Bill. *The Power of Identity: The Key to Personal and Professional Change.* Yellow Umbrella Press, January 2019

The link below will take you to a free EQ assessment from the Institute for Health and Human Potential. IHHP is a well-established and widely recognized source for EQ training and learning reinforcement.

https://www.ihhp.com/free-eq-quiz/

Mind Tools is a rich online portal for essential management, leadership and personal effectiveness skills. They have a wide range of high-quality, practical tools and resources including their free EQ assessment, which can be found through the link below:

https://www.mindtools.com/pages/article/ei-quiz.htm

The link below will take you to a comprehensive Emotional Intelligence resource, published by *Inc. Magazine*, titled: "15 Websites That Will Heighten Your Emotional Intelligence".

https://www.inc.com/marcel-schwantes/15-websites-that-will-make-your-emotional-intelligence-better.html

ABOUT THE AUTHORS

Melba J. Duncan is the Founder and President of The Duncan Group Inc., a retained recruiting and consulting firm, operating on a global basis. Since 1985, the firm has been advising CEOs and other corporate leaders regarding specialized senior management support resources. From 1976 to 1985, Ms. Duncan was Assistant to The Hon. Peter G. Peterson, Founder of The Peter G. Peterson Foundation, Chairman Emeritus and Co-Founder of The Blackstone Group, former Chairman and Chief Executive Officer of Lehman Brothers Kuhn Loeb Incorporated, and former Secretary of Commerce. In her prior position, she was Assistant to Sanford C. Bernstein, Chairman and Chief Executive Officer of Sanford C. Bernstein & Co., a New York Stock Exchange member firm, where she was elected Corporate Secretary and became a stockholder. Melba is the author of numerous books and articles, most notably the ground-breaking classic *The New Executive Assistant: Advice for Succeeding as an Executive or Administrative Assistant* (McGraw-Hill), and the highly-acclaimed *Harvard Business Review* articles 'The Case for Executive Assistants' and 'What Executive Assistants Know About Managing Up'.

Emily Schatz has been an Executive Assistant, Chief of Staff, and an Executive Support Leader since 2000, helping founders and global executives create and lead purpose-driven organizations. A graduate of Leadership Studies from Central Michigan University, she lives in Michigan with her partner, Chris, their two children, Elle and Rhys, and their Golden Retriever, Alex.

Tim Shea has gained extensive experience as a facilitator and coach, assisting leaders at all levels increase their ability to persuade, communicate and generate productive change. The true benefit of this work is in creating sustainable growth that meaningfully advance the organization's goals. He has regularly delivered training at the leadership development programs for GE, Honeywell, Lockheed, Invensys and for the NY State Excelsior Fellows academy.

Loretta Sophocleous is the Director of Executive Operations at TIAA where she reports to the CEO, Roger W. Ferguson, Jr. In this capacity, she provides strategic direction to the Office of the CEO. Loretta heads the C-Suite team of executive assistants to whom she provides mentoring, guidance and development opportunities. She is a member of the Seraphic Society and a founding member of C-SESP (C-Suite Executive Support Professionals), having served as their first President for six years. She now holds a seat on the Advisory Committee of that group. Prior to TIAA, she worked for the CEO of Deloitte Consulting in a similar role. She has worked at the C-Suite level for the last twenty years. She holds a bachelor's degree in Communications from City University of New York at Queens College and is a certified Insights Discovery facilitator.

Made in the USA
Las Vegas, NV
28 September 2021